After Effects
The Power
of Expression

François Lefebvre

ISBN: 978-0-578-40448-6

About
the author

François Lefebvre is a motion graphics artist based in New York City. With over a decade of experience in the industry, his flawless, unique style has led him to work for major companies and brands like Google, Amazon, Nike, Marvel, Paypal and the WWE among others. His expertise spans a broad range of digital/social media, broadcast media, and studio design.

Table of contents

Instructions

14 Value

14   Where can you find values?
15   4 types of values
16   Producing values
20   Applying values
21   Testing values

22 Mathematics

22   Arithmetic operators
23   Variables

24 Object

24   value
26   Objects contain values
26   Expression is an Object network
29   Follow The Object hierarchy
31   Rules of calling a value
     in an Object
34   Simplifying
35   Another way of
     calling a value in an Object
36   Link properties using Objects

37   Method
39   Argument
39   Simplifying even more

42 Syntax

42   Action
43   Semicolon
43   Statement
44   Expression contains statements
45   {Expression}
45   Unlimited space
46   Case sensitive
47   Camel case
47   Snake case
48   Comment
49   Left to right and top
     to bottom

50 Keywords

50   Using keywords to command
     the statements
50   var
51   if / else
53   How if / else works
54   A few keywords

Expressions

109 speedAtTime() and velocityAtTime()
110 Time remapping
113 sourceTime()

58	The power of index

58 Index number
59 For layer
59 For properties
60 For effect
61 The power of index
62 Property index
64 thisProperty
64 propertyGroup()
65 propertyIndex

70	Insight

70 Object
72 function()
77 Method
78 function() or object.method()
79 this

80	Length

80 Distance
81 Vector
83 length()
84 Create automatic behavior
   using distance
87 Interpolation methods
88 One layer to control them all
89 thiscomp.layer
   (thislayer,numberlayer)

92	Time

92 Generate animation using time
94 inPoint
95 outPoint
95 Duration
96 marker
98 Keyframe
99 nearestKey()
100 See values behind shapes
101 Math.cos() and Math.sin()
104 valueAtTime()
106 speed
108 velocity

114	Space

114 parent
116 toComp()
118 fromComp()
119 fromCompToSurface()

120	Control

121 Point Control
122 Color Control
125 Checkbox Control
127 Layer Control
129 Angle Control

132	Random

133 wiggle()
136 random()
137 seedRandom()
137 gaussRandom()
138 noise()
139 posterizeTime()

140	Condition

140 Boolean
141 Comparison operators
142 Keywords
142 if
143 if / else
143 Conditional ternary operator: ?
144 Logical operators
145 else if
146 switch
147 case
147 break
148 Assignment operators
149 Increment and decrement operators
150 while
152 do / while
153 for
154 continue
155 for / in

156   Express yourself

156   Text layer
156   Typing
157   sourceText
157   Character value
158   slice()
158   length
162   toLowerCase() and toUpperCase()
162   replace()
163   Global replacement

164   Loop

164   Saving time
164   Math.cos() and Math.sin()
165   % operator
166   Loop methods
167   loopOut()
168   You're ready

Bonus

176   New Expressions Engine:
**   JavaScript**

176   Multi-line String value
177   New methods for String values
178   New methods for Array values
180   var, let and const
183   Object constructor
184   Arrow functions
184   Default arguments
185   Rest and spread operators
186   Destructuring assignment
187   for / of
188   Test

Foreword

What is expression?
A simple language

Expression is the language that allows us to program or link various properties within Adobe After Effects. This coding language is written in ExtendScript, developed by Adobe, and is based on the JavaScript coding language. If you don't have any experience with coding in general, it can look scary and inaccessible, but believe me when I say that Expression is very logical. In fact, you'll only need to know a few terms to be able to read, write and decipher expressions. My goal in this book is to lighten things up, to show you that what may at first seem complex is ultimately a beautifully simple tool that will bring harmony to your project.

Who needs it?
Everyone

From apprentice to expert, this book is made for everyone who wishes to find inner peace in their workflow or project. In a fast-paced world where we need to produce more, collaborate with more people, integrate a ton of feedback and maintain consistency, while at the same time pushing to be more innovative, Expression is the ideal tool.

Have you ever heard of "the hidden grid behind a great design"? Expression can be this grid, one that will give your animation an invisible layer of inexplicable greatness. The advantage of working with Expression is that no matter whether you work in a team or by yourself, whether you're working on an existing project or building your own template, you still need to make your project clear and easily editable. Expression is the perfect language for communicating with other After Effects artists. Expression is a simple and powerful tool for everyone and everything, boosting your productivity so you'll have more time to spend on the most important task: being creative. Aside from this, it will also help you to better understand how After Effects works and use it to its full potential.

What do you need to know?
Nothing

I will assume that you have some familiarity with After Effects—the basics—but apart from this you don't need any knowledge of Expression, nor any other coding language. Beginning from a blank page, we'll cover everything. It's pretty straightforward, just codes and results. To be even more optimistic, I'd say you don't even need to know about After Effects to understand this book.

Why a book?
A complete course

Expression is a written language, so it's easier to focus by learning through reading than by watching a video tutorial.

The purpose of this book is for you to have a reference that allows you to swiftly search, learn, and review the terms necessary for you to use Expression in your daily After Effects workflow. Most of all, it's a complete course: by the end of this book, you'll have mastered a completely new language. How cool is that?

0   1080 px

0

All the examples
in this book will
be in a square
composition.

1080 px

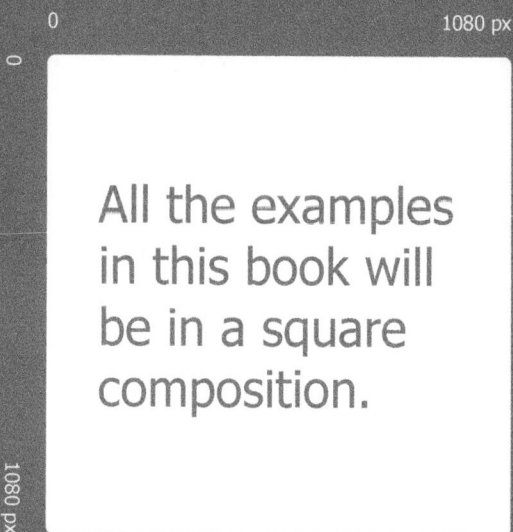

The grey boxes will be the expression editor, where we will write the expressions for
properties.

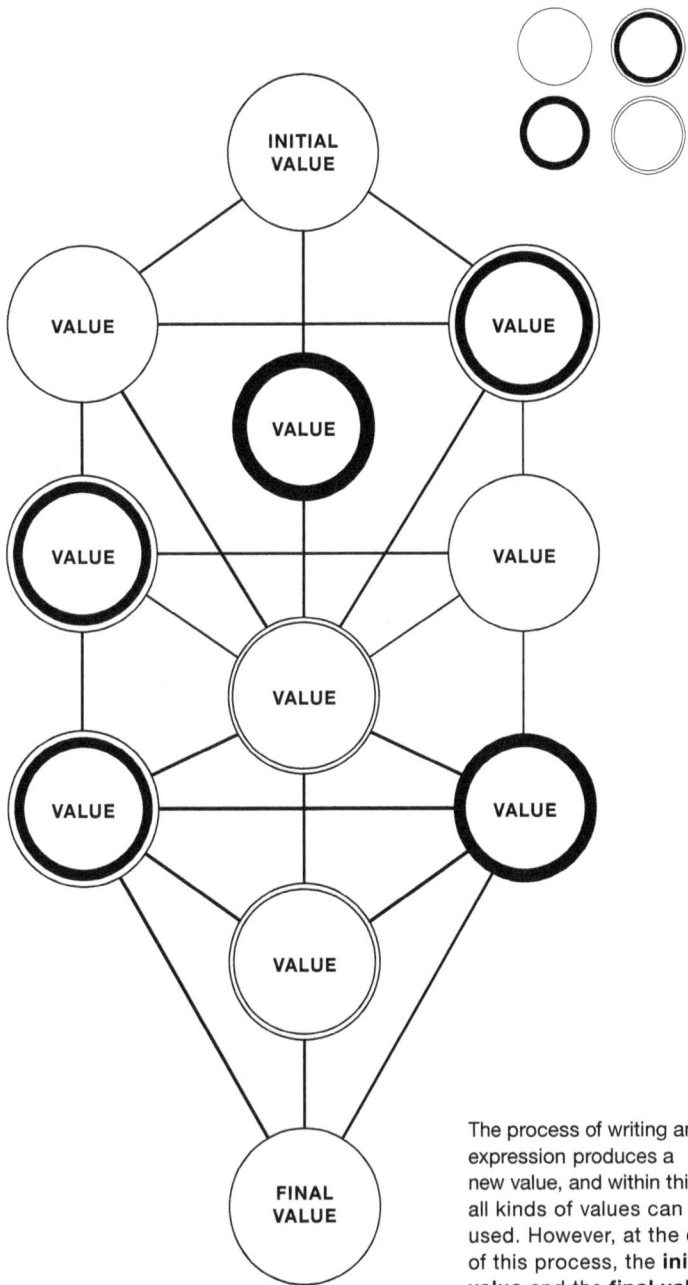

INITIAL
VALUE

VALUE

VALUE

VALUE

VALUE

VALUE

VALUE

VALUE

VALUE

VALUE

FINAL
VALUE

The process of writing an expression produces a new value, and within this all kinds of values can be used. However, at the end of this process, the **initial value** and the **final value** need to be of the same type.

Instructions

Value

The key point to understanding Expression is **value**; if you understand **value**, you'll be a master in Expression.

Where can you find values?

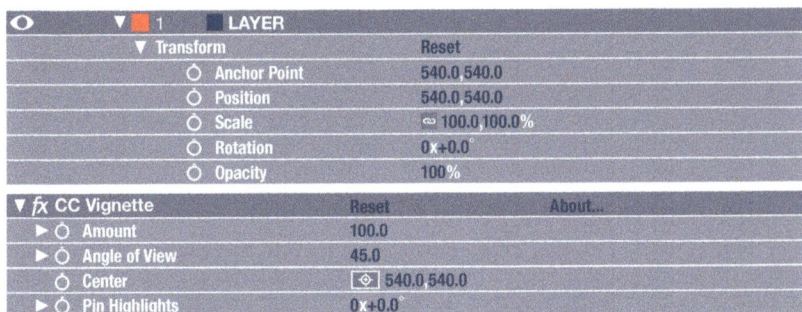

⊙	▼ ■ 1 ■ LAYER		
	▼ Transform	Reset	
	Ö Anchor Point	540.0 540.0	
	Ö Position	540.0 540.0	
	Ö Scale	∞ 100.0 100.0 %	
	Ö Rotation	0 x +0.0°	
	Ö Opacity	100 %	
	▼ fx CC Vignette	Reset	About...
	► Ö Amount	100.0	
	► Ö Angle of View	45.0	
	Ö Center	⊕ 540.0 540.0	
	► Ö Pin Highlights	0 x +0.0°	

PROPERTIES LAYER:

Anchor Point	540 pixels on the X-axis and 540 pixels on the Y-axis	2 values: 540 and 540
Position	540 pixels on the X-axis and 540 pixels on the Y-axis	2 values: 540 and 540
Scale	100% on the horizontal axis and 100% on the vertical axis	2 values: 100 and 100
Rotation	0 degree	1 value: 0
Opacity	100%	1 value: 100

PROPERTIES CC Vignette:

Amount	100	1 value: 100
Angle of View	45	1 value: 45
Center	540 pixels on the X-axis and 540 pixels on the Y-axis	2 values: 540 and 540
Pin Highlights	0	1 value: 0

All properties in After Effects are defined by values. For example, take a look at this Solid layer and CC Vignette effect. We can already see how we just determined two types: **Properties containing 1 value** and **properties containing 2 values.**

In fact, in Expression, certain units of measurement don't count: percentages of the Opacity property or degrees of the Rotation property. These values may not look the same, but in Expression they are the same type: each contain 1 value. The same is true for the Scale and Position properties: each contain 2 values. **In total, there are 4 types of values we need to know.**

4 types of values

Number value

Number value (also called **value**) is a single value: 12
It can also be a decimal: **12.5** (decimal numbers are written with a period in Expression)

String value

String value is the text value, and can be written between either single or double quotation marks:
"Text"
Or 'Text'
Or "This is a sentence."

Boolean value

Boolean value is a logical value: true or false

Array value

Array value is a group of values, written between square brackets with each value separated by a comma. It can contain as many values as you want:
[560,34] or [4,32,19,6]
It can also contain all the other types of values mentioned above, like String and Boolean values: [1,true,45,"Text"]
It can even contain Array values: [[13,45],[5,2]]

Train yourself
To recognize which type of value has a property.

PROPERTIES

Anchor Point	2 values: 540 and 540	Array value
Position	2 values: 540 and 540	Array value
Scale	2 values: 100 and 100	Array value
Rotation	1 value: 0	Number value
Opacity	1 value: 100	Number value
Amount	1 value: 100	Number value
Angle of View	1 value: 45	Number value
Center	2 values: 540 and 540	Array value
Pin Highlights	1 value: 0	Number value

Producing values

When you write an expression in a property, the goal is to produce a value. You'll only need to know four types of values to produce or use—keep this in mind and you won't need to deal with anything else. Now, let's produce these values:

In a new composition, let's add a **Text layer** and write **I AM A TEXT.**

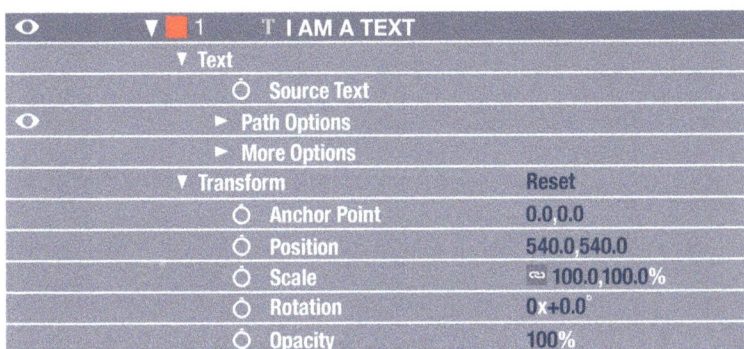

◉		▼ ■ 1	T I AM A TEXT	
		▼ Text		
			Ŏ Source Text	
◉			► Path Options	
			► More Options	
			▼ Transform	Reset
			Ŏ Anchor Point	0.0 0.0
			Ŏ Position	540.0 540.0
			Ŏ Scale	∞ 100.0 100.0%
			Ŏ Rotation	0x+0.0°
			Ŏ Opacity	100%

Note: all the properties with a stopwatch on their left side can be manipulated with an expression.

Let's open the expression editor of the Source Text property:
(**Animation** > **Add Expression** or **ALT + Click** on the stop watch)

By default, it should look like this:

```
text.sourceText
```

I AM A TEXT

Producing a number value

Now let's remove the default expression and add a number:

3

3

We just produced a **Number value**.
Let's add a decimal and see if it still works.

3.5

3.5

We just produced a decimal Number value; again, decimals in Expression are written with a period.

Producing a string value

OK, now let's see if we can add some text.

I AM A TEXT

Here is a new text

This produces an error message. This is because as I mentioned previously, a text value (or **String value**) needs to be written between single or double quotation marks.

"Here is a new text"

HERE IS A NEW TEXT

We just produced a **String value**.

Producing a Boolean value

Boolean values come in only two forms: **true** or **false**.

As we just saw with the **String value**, if you enter a random text without quotation marks, it will produce an error because Expression can't recognize text as values.

true	TRUE

When you write **true** or **false** it produces the value **true** or **false** without any error.
This is because **true** or **false** are actual values—like a Number value of 16 for example—and Expression treats them as values. They're essentially logical values that differentiate if what we write is **true** or **false**.

10<9	FALSE

10>9	TRUE

We just produced **Boolean values**;
these are values that can be interpreted
and used in Expression.

Producing an Array value

Now let's try to make an **Array value**:

9,7,12,5	5

This doesn't produce what we wanted. It only produces the last number, because as I mentioned an **Array value** needs to be between square brackets to produce a group of values.

[9,7,12,5]	9,7,12,5

We just produced an **Array value.**

Using an Array value with an Index number

An **Array value** is a group of values. The great thing about an **Array value** is that you can locate and select their values individually with an **Index number**. What's an **Index number**? It's the position of a value within a sequence of values. The important thing to remember about the Index number of an Array is that it's **zero-based**, meaning it begins the counting from 0, not from 1, so the first value in the Array value has the position 0. So, for this sequence:

[9,7,12,5]

Number value 9 is in position 0
Number value 7 is in position 1
Number value 12 is in position 2
Number value 5 is in position 3

[Array value][Index number]

Here's how we can use **Index numbers**: When we write a Number value between brackets after an Array value, it will use this number as an Index number to select which value to use in the Array value.

[9,7,12,5][0]	9	[9,7,12,5][2]	12	[9,7,12,5][4]	⚠
[9,7,12,5][1]	7	[9,7,12,5][3]	5		

Using 4 as an Index number will produce an error, because there is no value in position 4

In this example, you can see that we're using an Index number to locate and select a Number value within an Array value. We produced the Number value we selected, not an Array value. Note that **to produce a value** is the same as **to return a value**.

VALUE

0

Applying values

These are the four types of values that are recognized by Expression, and that's really not so many. The important thing to remember is that when you write an expression in a property, **the value you produce after the expression needs to be the same type as the initial value you had before the expression.**

Let's use the Solid layer from the previous example, and see how the initial values would look if we wrote their equivalent in Expression:

○	▼ ■ 1	■ LAYER			
	▼ Transform		Reset		
		○ Anchor Point	540.0 540.0		
		○ Position	540.0 540.0		
		○ Scale	100.0 100.0 %		
		○ Rotation	0 +0.0		
		○ Opacity	100 %		

PROPERTY	INITIAL VALUE	FINAL VALUE EXPECTED	EQUIVALENT
Anchor Point	2 values: 540 and 540	Array value	[540,540]
Position	2 values: 540 and 540	Array value	[540,540]
Scale	2 values: 100 and 100	Array value	[100,100]
Rotation	1 value: 0	Number value	0
Opacity	1 value: 100	Number value	100

You can use all four types of values to build an expression, but ultimately the one value you produce needs to be exactly the same type as the initial value: this is the key to Expression. If you don't produce the same type of value in a property, it will display an error message and won't work.

For example, if we write this in the expression editor of the rotation property of the layer:

[90,45,112] ⚠

This produces an error because the initial value of a rotation property is a Number value, and in our case we produced an Array value so it won't work. Instead, we need to produce a Number value.

[90,45,112][1]

Now it's working fine and produces 45, because we just used an Index number 1 to select the second Number value in the Array value, 45, producing a Number value. As you'll notice, we used an Array value to produce a Number value—remember, you can use any type of value in your expression as long as the final result is the same type of value as the initial one.

Testing values

At this point, when we produced a non-String value in the Source Text property, you're probably asking yourself why it doesn't produce an error. After all, this should be a String value, but we were able to produce all four types of values. This is because all the values you produce in the Source Text property will ultimately be converted into a String value:

Number Value	5	→	"5"	String Value
Array Value	[9,7,12,5]	→	"9,7,12,5"	String Value
Boolean Value	true	→	"true"	String Value

The great advantage of using a Text layer is that it accepts all four types of values—this is how we can see these values displayed in the frame. When I'm writing an expression, I like to use a Text layer as a universal values tool to see what I'm manipulating, so I can test and see the result of my expressions as text and be sure I'm on the right track. Throughout this book, we will be using the Text layer to display the results of the expressions (or parts of them); while expressions can be easy to see when they're simple, when they get a little more complex it helps to keep track of what's going on. Just as a programmer would use a debugger to test their code, we'll use the Text layer to do the same.

Recap focus

Number value	2, 4, 2.4, 189, ...
String value	"TEXT", 'SENTENCE TEXT 2', 'ANOTHER TEXT', ...
Boolean value	true or false
Array value	[33,55], [989,23,12], [1,true,23,"text"], ...

Mathematics

The great thing about Expression—and what makes it so easy to work with—is that it uses the basics of Mathematics to manipulate values, and you certainly don't even need to be a genius at Math to use it.

Arithmetic operators

Let's go to the Source Text property of a Text layer and do a little simple Math with Number values:

+ Addition   ***** Multiplication

- Subtraction   **/** Division

10+5 → 15

(10+5)*2 → 30

120/2 → 60

and ( ) parentheses **(not an operator.)**

Variables

Just as in basic Math, you can create variables and make regular equations. Creating a variable can be useful to store a value and reuse it somewhere else in the expression.

```
x=10;
x+10;
```

20

Three rules with variables

1

variable = value
~~value = variable~~

Creating a variable is called "assigning a value", and it works by putting the variable first, then the value you want to assign to it. It doesn't work the other way around.

2

= is not ==

The equals sign operator in Expression is ==; the = sign is the assignment operator. One equals sign is used to create a variable, two equal signs are used to compare values. Let me demonstrate this:

```
x = 10;
x == 11;
```

FALSE

First, we create a variable x, to which we assign the Number value 10. We then compare x to the Number value 11 using the equal sign operator == ; as you can see, when we compare the two it produces a Boolean value saying it's false.

```
x = 10;
x = 11;
```

11

First we assign the Number value 10 to x, but then we re-assign the Number value 11 to x. This ultimately produces 11, as this is the last value that we assigned to x.

3

variable2 = 10
~~2variable = 10~~

You can use any letter, word, upper or lower case and with numbers to create the name of the variable. However, you of course can't begin with a number or simply name it as a number, as we saw in rule 1.

Object

Working with Expression means working with values. You can generate these by writing them, but you can also locate, link and manipulate them using built-in terms.

value

Properties are defined by values, but the word **value** is also a term that can be used and interpreted by Expression to produce the value of the property at the current time where the current expression lives.

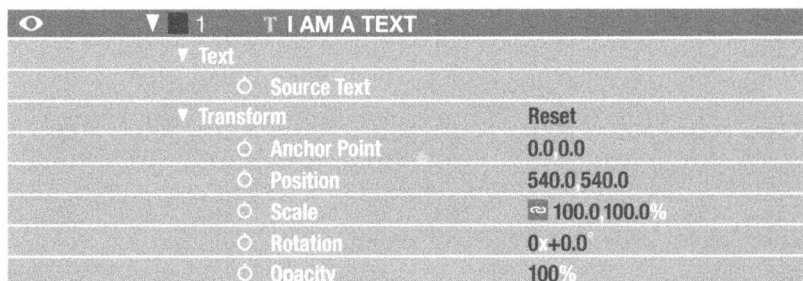

O	▼ ■ 1	T I AM A TEXT	
	▼ Text		
		O Source Text	
	▼ Transform		Reset
		O Anchor Point	0.0 0.0
		O Position	540.0 540.0
		O Scale	⌘ 100.0 100.0%
		O Rotation	0 +0.0
		O Opacity	100%

Let's re-use the Text layer "I AM A TEXT" and write the term **value** in the Source Text property:

value		I AM A TEXT

The term **value** works the same way in any property. The values that you can manually change before using Expression are called **parametric values** (in blue).

PROPERTY	PARAMETRIC VALUE	EXPRESSION	RESULT
Anchor Point	0.0,0.0	value	[0,0]
Position	540.0,540.0	value	[540,540]
Scale	100,100	value	[100,100]
Rotation	0x+0.0	value	0
Opacity	100	value	100

▼ At Current Time

◇	▼ ■ 1	T I AM A TEXT			
◀ ◇ ▶	▼ Transform		Reset		
		○ ⌊∠ Position	742.5 865.1	◀	◀▶

Position	742.5,865.1	value	[742.5,865.1]

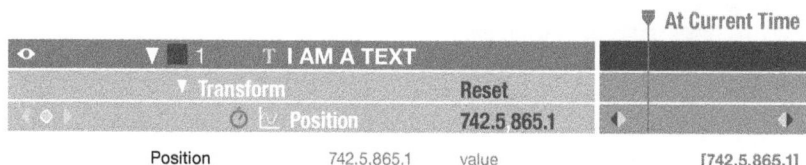

After seeing the behavior of the value term, there are two things we can generalize:

1. Expression happens last

Writing the term **value** is great because it allows us to reuse the parametric value of the property where we write the expression, thus producing the value of the property before the expression. It's important to understand that Expression always happens last in the process of calculation within After Effects; for each frame, after evaluating the value of the property, After Effects operates the expression written within the property.

2. Expression lives on its own

This built-in term also allows us to establish another rule in Expression. As we can see, the term **value** will produce a different value if you write it in the rotation property as when you write it in the scale property. Everything that you write in the expression editor of a property only exists in the expression editor of that particular property, not outside. The term **value** will produce different values according to which property you write it in; similarly, an expression lives on its own.

Thanks to the term **value**, we can access the initial (or parametric) value of the property where we write the expression. This is rather useful, but the best part of writing an expression is the ability to use the values of other properties, creating interactions between them. We'll now look at how to access these other properties in order to use them, and to do this we need to see what doors can be opened by other built-in terms.

Objects contain values

value is a term that can be used in Expression—it produces the value of the current property. In Expression, these properties are called Objects and they contain the values.

```
OBJECT
Anchor Point    •————————•  value
Position        •————————•  value
Scale           •————————•  value
Rotation        •————————•  value
Opacity         •————————•  value
```

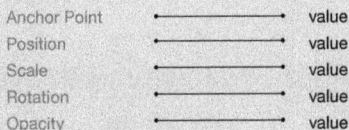

Properties in After Effects
are **Objects** in Expression.

Expression is an Object network

To clearly understand how to use the built-in terms available in Expression and thus be able to locate other values, you first have to visualize a hierarchy in Expression, one that is made from **Objects**. For example, we know that these properties are located in the layer, which is also an **Object**.

```
OBJECT              OBJECT
Layer   •————————•  Anchor Point    •————————•  value
                    Position        •————————•  value
                    Scale           •————————•  value
                    Rotation        •————————•  value
                    Opacity         •————————•  value
```

The **Objects** contain values but they can also contain other **Objects**.

Expression is an Object network, so everything you find in the After Effects hierarchy is an **Object**.

We know that an **Object** can be layers (Camera, Solid Layer, Light, Footage) and since we know that effects contain properties with values, this means an effect is also an **Object** that contains other **Objects**.

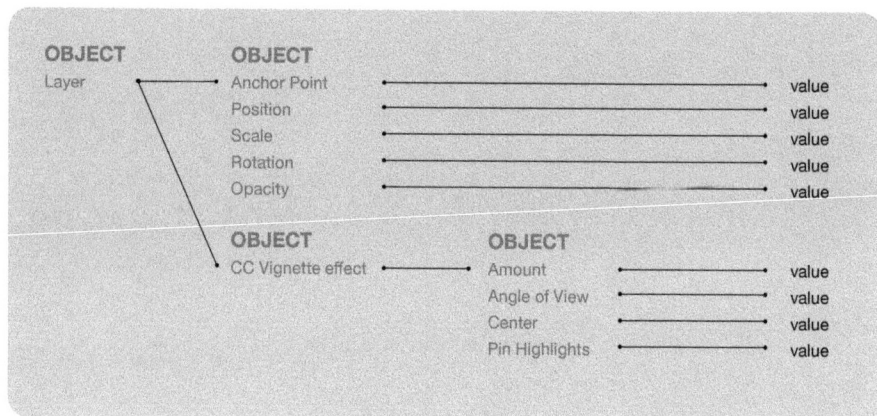

```
OBJECT          OBJECT
Layer           Anchor Point  •————————————————————•  value
                Position      •————————————————————•  value
                Scale         •————————————————————•  value
                Rotation      •————————————————————•  value
                Opacity       •————————————————————•  value

                OBJECT              OBJECT
                CC Vignette effect •——————•  Amount        •——————•  value
                                             Angle of View •——————•  value
                                             Center        •——————•  value
                                             Pin Highlights •——————•  value
```

Objects are groups - they contain values, but as we've just seen with the effect inside the layer, they can also contain other **Objects**. For example, most **Objects** will almost always be inside another larger **Object**: the Composition.

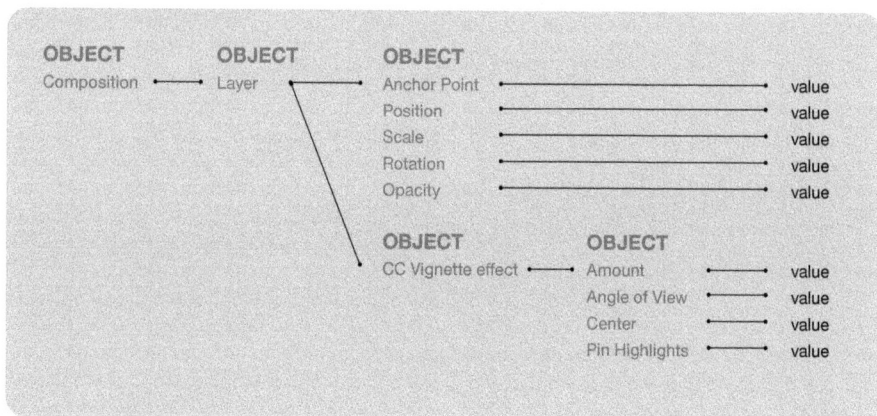

```
OBJECT          OBJECT          OBJECT
Composition •——• Layer •——————• Anchor Point  •————————————————————•  value
                                Position      •————————————————————•  value
                                Scale         •————————————————————•  value
                                Rotation      •————————————————————•  value
                                Opacity       •————————————————————•  value

                                OBJECT              OBJECT
                                CC Vignette effect •——• Amount        •————•  value
                                                       Angle of View •————•  value
                                                       Center        •————•  value
                                                       Pin Highlights •————•  value
```

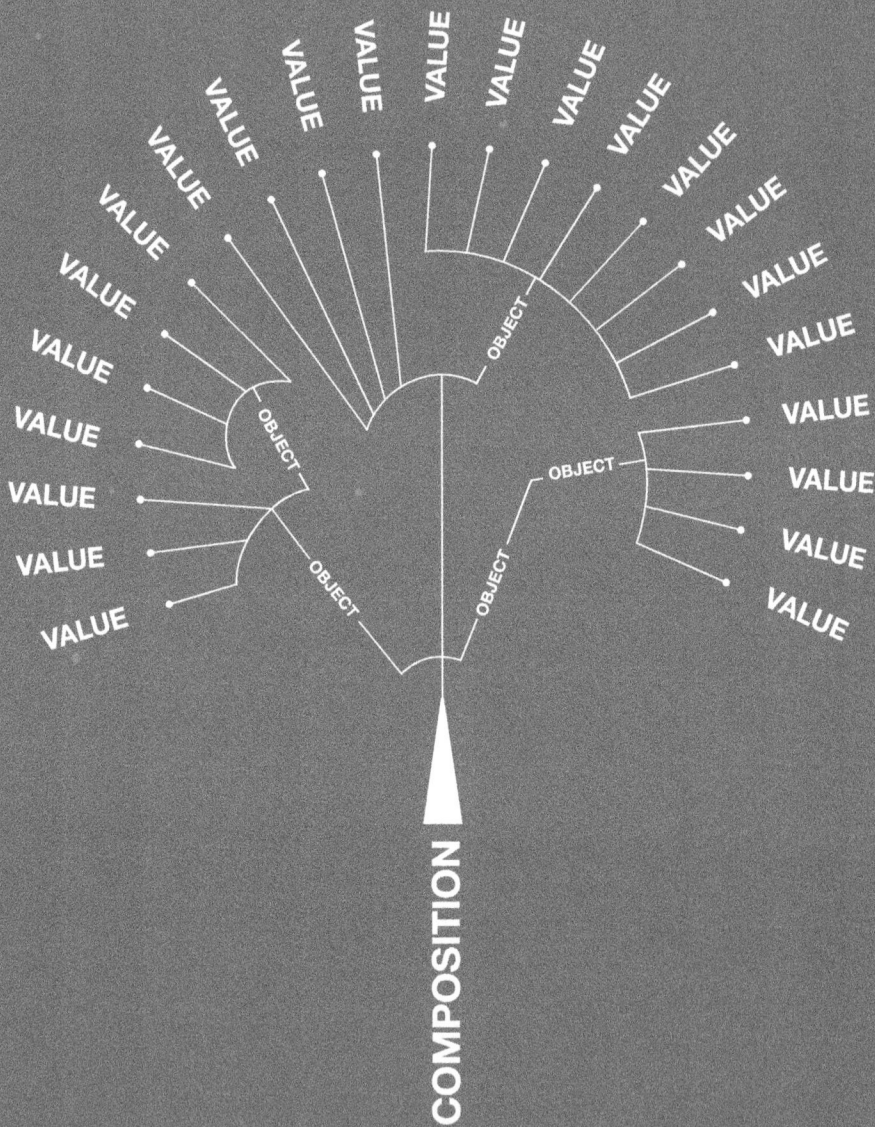

VALUE
VALUE
VALUE
VALUE
VALUE
VALUE
VALUE
VALUE
VALUE
VALUE
VALUE
VALUE
VALUE
VALUE
VALUE

VALUE
VALUE
VALUE
VALUE
VALUE
VALUE
VALUE
VALUE

OBJECT

OBJECT

OBJECT

OBJECT

OBJECT

COMPOSITION

- ● Composition
- ● Object
- ● Object
- ○ Value

Follow the Object hierarchy

Locating a value in Expression essentially functions like a directory in a computer - you work from the biggest folder to the smallest:

Composition > Object > Object > Value

So, we now want to see how to call the value of a property from one layer to the property of another layer.

Let's add a Solid layer under the Text layer.

●		► ■ 1	T I AM A TEXT	
●		▼ ■ 2	■ Red Solid	
		▼ Transform		Reset
		Ò Anchor Point		540.0 540.0
		Ò Position		540.0 540.0
		Ò Scale		⊂⊃ 100.0 100.0 %
		Ò Rotation		0 +0.0
		Ò Opacity		100 %

I'd like the value of the opacity property of the Red Solid layer to be displayed on screen through the Text layer, so let's open the expression editor of the **Source Text property** of the Text layer:

thisComp

[OBJECT COMP]

This produces the main Object,
which is the composition we are working on.

thisComp.layer("Red Solid")

[OBJECT LAYER]

This produces the Object layer from
which we want the opacity property.

thisComp.layer("Red Solid").transform

[OBJECT GROUP]

The opacity property is inside one other Object—
the transform group—which is itself in the Object layer.
We're getting closer.

thisComp.layer("Red Solid").transform.opacity

100

*Note: In some of the latest versions of After Effects, the [OBJECT COMP],
[OBJECT LAYER] and [OBJECT GROUP] may be displayed respectively
as [OBJECT OBJECT], Red Solid and Transform.*

Now, if we change the opacity of the Solid layer, we can see it automatically
updates in the Text layer.

0

50

75

100

Let's review the expression:

thisComp.layer("Red Solid").transform.opacity

OBJECT COMP   OBJECT LAYER   OBJECT GROUP   PROPERTY

Rules of calling a value in an Object

Left to right

When you call the value of a property, you start by writing in order of size, from the biggest to the smallest object containers, until you reach the property - from left to right.

Separated by a period

The different terms need to be separated by a period.

Object

OBJECT COMP: The main Object, which includes everything is the composition we are currently working on. If we call the composition that we're working on, we can write **thisComp**; if we want the value from another composition, we have to write **comp("name")**

OBJECT LAYER: This is the Solid layer. If we call the layer that we're working on, we can write **thisLayer**, without having to call the Object Comp before; if we want the value from another layer, we have to write **layer("name")**

If you want to call another composition or layer, the name that's between parentheses works as a String value, so you have to put the name between single or double quotation marks: comp('name') or layer("name")

OBJECT GROUP: The transform Object group contains the properties of the layer.

PROPERTY: Finally, the property contains the value.

Object comp, Object layer, Object group and Property are not different things, they're the same: an Object that contains something, so there's no need to differentiate between them:

thisComp.layer("Red Solid").transform.opacity

OBJECT   OBJECT   OBJECT   OBJECT

To find where a value is located, you just have to follow the hierarchy
of the layer when you reveal the Objects.

O		►	1	T I AM A TEXT	
O		▼	2	■ Red Solid	
		▼ Transform			Reset
		○ Anchor Point			540.0 540.0
		○ Position			540.0 540.0
		○ Scale			100.0 100.0%
		○ Rotation			0 x +0.0
		○ Opacity			100 %

Now let's try to display the position value of the Red Solid layer
to see if this also works:

thisComp.layer("Red Solid").transform.position

[OBJECT
PROPERTY]

This didn't produce what we expected, because we called the position value of the Red
Solid layer to a Source Text value. We know that a position value has an Array value, so
in **Expression an Array value works like an Object**. If you link two properties with an
Array value this will work fine, but otherwise we need to be more specific, because our
expression didn't specify what we wanted from this Object.

thisComp.layer("Red Solid").transform.position.value

540,540

When you specify the term **value** after an Object, it means that you want to call the
value of the object, not the object itself. Adding the term **value** after calling an Object will
always work. Sometimes you don't need to add this term, for example when the property
has a Number value. In some of the latest versions of After Effects the term **value** for a
property with an Array value doesn't need to be added either, although it never hurts to
be too specific.

The position property has an Array value because it has two values—it's a group of values. Remember we can select these values individually when they are followed by an Array Index number:

thisComp.layer("Red Solid").transform.position.value[0]

540

thisComp.layer("Red Solid").transform.position.value[1]

540

Instead of using **value**, you can also call the name of the Object by adding the term **name** to the Object.

thisComp.layer("Red Solid").transform.position.name

POSITION

An Object can produce its **value** or its **name**.

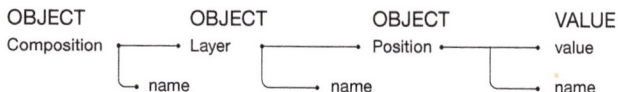

OBJECT	OBJECT	OBJECT	VALUE
Composition	Layer	Position	value
name	name		name

Note that if you don't specify what value you want to produce from the Object property by using **name** or **value**, it will produce the **value** by default..

rotation   is the same as   rotation.value

Simplifying

The great thing about Expression is that you can simplify your expressions; if you don't call the biggest Object container or the Object containers that follow, it will assume that the one you want is the Object where the expression lives. We saw this at the beginning of this chapter with the term **value**. When we just wrote **value**, it assumed that we wanted the value of the property inside the layer and inside the actual composition where the expression was written. So if you don't specify, Expression will fill in the blank for you and select the missing part. By using this technique, we can simplify our expressions.

Let's return to the Text layer—still in the Source Text property—
and try to show the position value of the Text layer,
which should be:

thisComp.layer("I AM A TEXT").transform.position.value

540,540

As we saw previously, when we use the current composition, we can write the Object **thisComp** instead of writing **comp("name")**. We can also do this if we want to use the layer where the expression lives; instead of writing **layer("name")** we can use the Object **thisLayer**. If we do this we don't even need to specify the composition, because Expression will assume that the current composition is the one where we want to write the expression. This also works if we don't specify the layer, because it will assume that we want to use the layer where the expression lives.

Below are the various differerent ways we could have called the value to produce the same result:

comp("name").layer("I AM A TEXT").transform.position.value

thisComp.layer("I AM A TEXT").transform.position.value

thisLayer.transform.position.value

thisLayer.position.value

transform.position.value

position.value

Another way of calling a value in an Object

This is not very common, but you may encounter it. Just as in our last example, this would produce the same result.

object.value = object["value"]

position.value

position["value"]

Link properties using Objects

Now that we can display the position value of the Text layer, let's link this value to the position value of the Red Solid layer to see the real advantage of Expression.

Remember, the Text layer is still displaying its own position value.

Let's open the expression editor of the position property of the Red Solid layer and write this:

[800,800]

540,540

As you'll remember, this is how we write an Array value when we have a group of values; position is a vector, and it has two dimensions, so it needs an Array value:

$$[x,y]$$

The first value will be the x coordinate and the second will be the y coordinate. This expression overwrites the parametric value of the position object. The position value of the Red Solid layer is 800 on x and 800 on y.

In the position property of the Text layer, let's write:

thisComp.layer("Red Solid").position

800,800

As we can now see, the Text layer displays that its position is [800,800] - exactly the same as the Red Solid layer - which means that the position of the Text layer is linked to the Red Solid layer and will have the same position value. To be certain, let's remove the expression in the position property of the Red Solid layer and then move it manually, to see if the Text layer maintains the same position.

312,324

762,418

540,706

302,874

Method

As you'll see when you move the Red Solid layer with your mouse, the Text layer will follow, and it displays the same current position as the Red Solid layer. You may also notice that it will sometimes display Number values with a lot of decimals.

.23094,504.9

Let's say we want to have something cleaner, to round off the Number values to a whole number. Let's open the expression editor of the position property of the Red Solid layer and write this:

[Math.round(position[0]),Math.round(position[1])]

495,505

The values are now rounded out to whole numbers because we've used a built-in **method** term—**Math.round()**—to produce it..

Let's review the expression:

As you'll remember, the position property needs an Array value, so it looks like this:

[x,y]

If we want to access and use the parametric values of the position property, we can write this in the expression editor:

> position

We have an expression on this property, which produces the parametric values of the position object, just as if we were to write **value**. We used an expression on this property, but we're still able to manually control the position of the layer. Remember, we can also individually call a value in an Array value with the Array Index number, which can be split so that it looks like a position value [x,y]:

> [position[0],position[1]]

> [position[0],position[1]]   is the same as   position

By doing this, we have an individual control for each dimension.
Now it's time to introduce the **method**, which, is a term that produces a new value.

We just saw a **method** that can round a decimal Number value to the nearest whole Number value, namely **Math.round()**:

Math.round(Number value)

> Math.round(1.1)   1   Math.round(1.8)   2

Math.round() works only with a **Number value**, not directly with an **Array value**, but because we were able to split our **Array value** into individual **Number values**, we can use this method:

> **[Math.round(position[0]),Math.round(position[1])]**

Argument

The value that you need to enter between the parentheses of a method is called the **Argument** (it is also known as the **Parameter**).

Math.round**(value)**
Object.Method**(Argument)**

Methods are Objects inside another Object. Methods produce a new value, but they also behave like a regular Object, so they can contain Objects and values.

Simplifying even more

Earlier on, we saw that we can create a variable and assign a value to it. You can also assign an Object to a variable to pass along a value. Here is another way we could have written the expression using variables:

```
x = position[0];
y = position[1];

[Math.round(x),Math.round(y)];
```

This looks much more readable, and you'll see that the simpler you keep the expression as it gets is more advanced, the easier it will be to handle and edit.

We can simplify this even more by using only one variable:

```
x = position.value;
[Math.round(x[0]),Math.round(x[1])];
```

or

```
x = position;
[Math.round(x[0]),Math.round(x[1])];
```

To recap, we've seen how we can use built-in terms to locate, pass and manipulate values from After Effects properties. We can now establish two different type of terms:

Object built-in terms

Compositions, layers, effects, properties and methods are Objects in Expression. An Object can contain values, as well as other Objects.

Value built-in terms

Because an Object usually has several values, you need to know which one to use. For example, the terms **value** and **name** produce values from Objects. These built-in terms are also called properties or attributes of the Object.

At the end of this book you'll find a condensed list of built-in terms you can use.

Visualizing this map with some of the built-in objects and values can give you a clearer idea of the Object network in Expression, as well as how to call objects and values when building an expression.

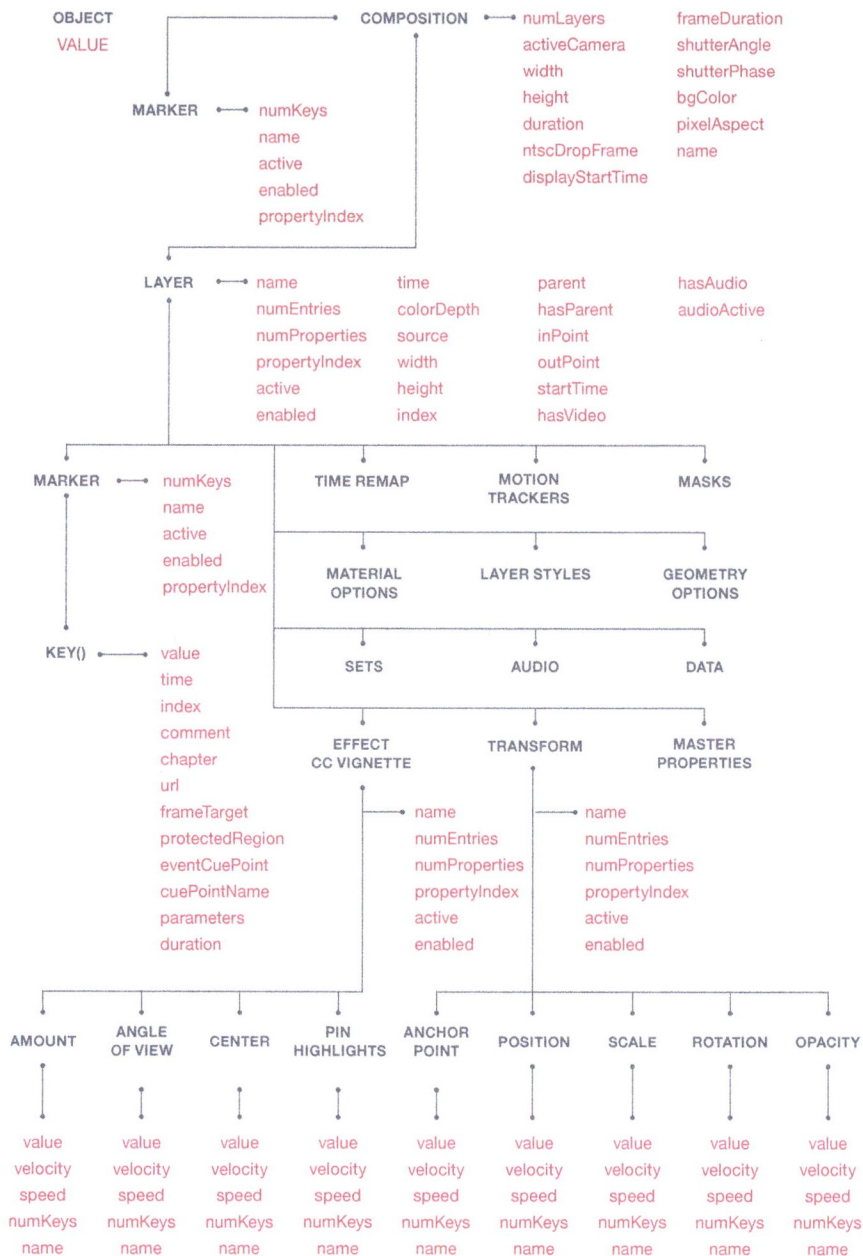

OBJECT
VALUE

COMPOSITION → numLayers   frameDuration
activeCamera   shutterAngle
width   shutterPhase
height   bgColor
duration   pixelAspect
ntscDropFrame   name
displayStartTime

MARKER → numKeys
name
active
enabled
propertyIndex

LAYER → name   time   parent   hasAudio
numEntries   colorDepth   hasParent   audioActive
numProperties   source   inPoint
propertyIndex   width   outPoint
active   height   startTime
enabled   index   hasVideo

MARKER → numKeys
name
active
enabled
propertyIndex

TIME REMAP   **MOTION TRACKERS**   **MASKS**

KEY() → value
time
index
comment
chapter
url
frameTarget
protectedRegion
eventCuePoint
cuePointName
parameters
duration

MATERIAL OPTIONS   **LAYER STYLES**   **GEOMETRY OPTIONS**

SETS   **AUDIO**   **DATA**

EFFECT CC VIGNETTE   **TRANSFORM**   **MASTER PROPERTIES**

name   name
numEntries   numEntries
numProperties   numProperties
propertyIndex   propertyIndex
active   active
enabled   enabled

AMOUNT	ANGLE OF VIEW	CENTER	PIN HIGHLIGHTS	ANCHOR POINT	POSITION	SCALE	ROTATION	OPACITY
value	value	value	value	value	value	value	value	value
velocity	velocity	velocity	velocity	velocity	velocity	velocity	velocity	velocity
speed	speed	speed	speed	speed	speed	speed	speed	speed
numKeys	numKeys	numKeys	numKeys	numKeys	numKeys	numKeys	numKeys	numKeys
name	name	name	name	name	name	name	name	name

Syntax

Like every language, Expression has its own grammar, but contrary to what you might think there is a great deal more freedom and creativity to writing it than meets the eye. Remember that my goal here is to lighten things up, to show that the syntax of the language is really not so rigorous—in fact, this is an essential part of your acceptance to use Expression in your everyday workflow. We'll see that the only limitation is how much space you feel you can allow yourself.

Action

In the last chapter, we created an expression to round out the position values of a layer to whole numbers:

```
x = position[0];
y = position[1];

[Math.round(x),Math.round(y)];
```

The first thing you'll notice is that we have three distinct lines; actually, instead of calling it a line, let's call it an **Action**.

Action 1:
x = position[0];

We create a variable x that we assign to the x parametric position value.

Action 2:
y = position[1];

We create a variable y that we assign to the y parametric position value.

Action 3:
[Math.round(x),Math.round(y)];

We create an Array value containing two values, namely the two rounded out values from the x and y variables produced by the Math.round() method.

Semicolon

We then notice that all the actions finish with a **semicolon**. In Expression, this is the punctuation that marks the end of an action, like a period in a sentence. The **action** can stand on one line or multiple lines—only the presence of the **semicolon** will finish the **action**. This means that we don't really need to fit everything onto one line, so we aren't limited by visual constraints.

These are all the same:

```
x = position[0];
```

```
x =
position[0];
```

```
x =
position
[0];
```

```
x =
position
[0]
;
```

Statement

Finally, the general denomination for this unit, is called a **statement**.
A **statement** can call or produce a value. A **statement** in Expression is an action that ends with a semicolon.

```
x = position[0];
```

Expression contains statements

So far in this book, we've been able to write the expressions in one statement, without adding a **semicolon** at the end. When you have one statement, Expression will read the expression and is able to see where it starts and stops. But when you have more than one statement, you'll need to make sure that the semicolon is at the end of each one.

```
x = position[0] y = position[1] [Math.round(x),Math.round(y)]
```

⚠️

```
x = position[0]; y = position[1]; [Math.round(x),Math.round(y)];
```

So as you can see the **semicolon** is an indication for Expression to know where the statement starts and stops. You don't really need to add it if you only have one statement in an expression, or at the end of the last statement in an expression that contains several statements.

```
x = position[0]
```

```
x = position[0];
```

The presence of the semicolon is optional when the statement is single or the last in a series.

```
x = position[0];
y = position[1];
[Math.round(x),Math.round(y)]
```

```
x = position[0];
y = position[1];
[Math.round(x),Math.round(y)];
```

For our own discipline, we'll try to always write the **semicolon** when possible.

```
x = position[0];
y = position[1];
[Math.round(x),Math.round(y)];
```

Together, the group of statements form an expression.

An expression can be one statement or several statements—it's the entire unit that forms the expression.

{Expression}

An expression is made up of single or multiple statements between curly brackets. The curly brackets start and finish the expression. You don't need to add a semicolon to close a single statement, just as when you write a single expression in the expression editor, you don't need to write the expression inside curly brackets—it will be assumed by the expression editor.

```
{x = position[0];}
```

```
x = position[0];
```

```
{x = position[0];
y = position[1];
[Math.round(x),Math.round(y)];}
```

```
x = position[0];
y = position[1];
[Math.round(x),Math.round(y)];
```

Unlimited space

We've seen that we're not limited by fitting everything onto one line to make a **statement**. The same is true for general space, even between terms, variables, operators or punctuations.

```
x = thisLayer.position[0];
y = thisLayer.position[1];
[Math.round(x),Math.round(y)];
```

```
x = thisLayer . position  [0]

;
y=    thisLayer . position [1]  ;
```

As much space
as you like

```
[ Math . round (x) , Math.    round
(y) ]  ;
```

You don't have to worry about how much space you take up when you write an expression—you can space it out a lot or keep it tight, it's purely a case of what's most comfortable to your eyes. But let's not forget that Expression is a language, and keeping it tidy can be of great benefit for you when making revisions later on; it can also be useful if someone else picks up your project, as they'll be able to immediately edit your work. Usually, maintaining compact and consistent spacing is the favored option in the world of Expression users, as in the example, above left.

Case sensitive

It's good to know we have choices, but when we take a closer look, we'll notice that some of the words have capital letters and others do not. This will be one of our only constraints. Expression is a **Case Sensitive** language and can recognize the difference between upper and lower case letters, so you do need to write the built-in terms correctly.

```
Position;
```

```
position;
```

```
math.round(1.2);
```

```
Math.round(1.2);
```

When calling a variable you created, make sure you follow the **Case Sensitive** rule.

```
x=thisLayer.position[0];
y=thisLayer.position[1];

[Math.round(X),Math.round(y)];
```

```
x=thisLayer.position[0];
y=thisLayer.position[1];

[Math.round(x),Math.round(y)];
```

```
X=thisLayer.position[0];
y=thisLayer.position[1];

[Math.round(X),Math.round(y)];
```

Camel case

Another term we've seen is the object **thisLayer**.

```
x=thislayer.position[0];
```

⚠️

```
x=thisLayer.position[0];
```

Writing like this, where you break up two words not with a space but by writing the second word with an upper case letter, is called **Camel Case**. Usually, built-in terms made of two words in Expression are written in Camel Case, like **thisComp** or **thisLayer**. When going over expressions, such as this one, here is a common way to name a variable:

```
xVariable=thisLayer.position[0];
y=thisLayer.position[1];

[Math.round(xVariable),Math.round(y)];
```

You'll notice that I named my variable using a **Camel Case**, but this is arbitrary—I could also have written it like this:

```
xvariable=thisLayer.position[0];
y=thisLayer.position[1];

[Math.round(xvariable),Math.round(y)];
```

It's up to you how you create a variable—it will work just the same, it's again a case of maintaining harmony. It's good to be consistent, and it's easier if you want to make it readable by someone else, but it's good to know it won't cause an error if your variable doesn't use **Camel Case**.

Snake case

Just so you know, some Expression users also create their variables like this:

myComp   my_comp

myLayer   my_layer

Comment

While we're talking about making things more readable, for you or others who might use your expression, it's useful to know you can add comments in Expression.

```
xVariable=thisLayer.position[0]; // This variable is Camel Case
yvariable=thisLayer.position[1]; // This variable is not Camel Case

[Math.round(xVariable),Math.round(yvariable)];
```

Writing comments means you can write whatever you want, in a realm where the rules of Expression's language are temporarily suspended. There are two ways to write comment. You can write it on a line using two slashes followed by your comment, using any characters or language (even emojis), but it needs to be on the same line and to the right of what you are commenting on. It can also be on a line by itself.

```
xVariable=thisLayer.position[0];
//This variable above is Camel Case
yvariable=thisLayer.position[1]; // This variable is not Camel Case

[Math.round(xVariable),Math.round(yvariable)];
```

The second way to write a comment is to fit it onto multiple lines, beginning with /* and ending with */ —everything in between won't be readable by the expression editor.

```
xVariable=thisLayer.position[0]; /* This variable
above is
Camel Case */

yvariable=thisLayer.position[1]; // This variable is not Camel Case  😊
[Math.round(xVariable),Math.round(yvariable)];
```

// COMMENT ON ONE LINE
/* COMMENT
ON MULTIPLE
LINES */

Left to right and top to bottom

Earlier we saw that to create a variable, we need to first write the variable then assign an object or a value to it:

variable = object or value

The software reads the expressions from left to right; in the same way, when you have multiple statements in your expression, it will read them from top to bottom, which means **the last statement within the expression will be the last action performed.**

```
x = position[0];
y = position[1];

[Math.round(x),Math.round(y)];
[800,800];
```

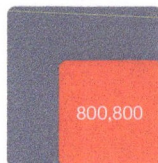
800,800

The Red Solid layer will be locked at [800,800] for the position value, because the final value produced is the last statement written in the expression editor: [800,800]. The other statements written before this one will be read and performed, but they will then be overwritten by the last statement. For example, these two expressions will produce the exact same result:

```
x = position[0];
y = position[1];

[Math.round(x),Math.round(y)];

[800,800];
```

=

```
[800,800];
```

Keywords

So far, we've seen that we can create an expression with Values, Mathematic operators, Objects, and Comments. The last one we'll add to this list is Keywords.

Using keywords to command the statements

We've seen that an expression can have one or several statements. A statement can call or produce a value.

Keywords are here to manipulate the statements. Keywords are placed before the statement, and provide instructions on to how to use the statement.

Keyword + Statement;

---

var

Earlier in the book, we have seen that to create a variable, we need to write the variable first then the value. Like in this example:

```
x = 10;
```

Another way to create a variable is using the keyword **var**:

```
var x = 10;
```

var nameVariable = value;

Since Expression borrows some of its language from JavaScript, there are some sub-tleties that can be *assumed* but not necessarily *known*. A variable without var is called a Global variable, **var** can be a Global variable but in certain case can become a Local vari-able. For the purpose of our mission we won't need to worry about this. **var** is a keyword, it's one of the few keywords you will encounter.

if / else

👁	▼ ■ 1	T I AM A TEXT		
	▼ Text			
		Ò Source Text		
👁		► Path Options		
		► More Options		
		▼ Transform	Reset	
		Ò Anchor Point	0.0 0.0	
		Ò Position	540.0 540.0	
		Ò Scale	⊖ 100.0 100.0%	
		Ò Rotation	0x +0.0	
		Ò Opacity	100%	
👁	▼ ■ 2	■ Red Solid		
		▼ Transform	Reset	
		Ò Anchor Point	540.0 540.0	
		Ò Position	540.0 540.0	
		Ò Scale	⊖ 100.0 100.0%	
		Ò Rotation	0x +0.0	
		Ò Opacity	100%	

Now I want the Text layer to display its actual rotation value, so to do this I'll write in the expression editor of the Source Text property:

```
thisLayer.rotation.value;
```

or in a simpler way

```
rotation;
```

This displays the value of the rotation property of the Text layer.

Now I want to link the rotation property of the Text layer to the rotation property of the Red Solid layer, so that the Red Solid layer controls the rotation of the Text layer. To do this, let's write in the expression editor of the rotation property of the Text layer:

```
thisComp.layer("Red Solid").rotation;
```

We can see that when we rotate the Red Solid layer, the Text layer is linked, so it has the same rotation value. Now, how about if we want the Text layer to have an opacity of 100% when the rotation is between 0 and 90 degrees, then change to 50% when it passes 90 degrees.

To do this, we'll have to write an expression in the Opacity property of the Text layer but first I want my Text layer to also display its own opacity value. Let's write this in the Source Text property of the Text layer:

```
r = rotation.value; // This is the rotation value of the layer
o = opacity.value; // This is the opacity value of the layer

"rotation: " + r + "\r" + "opacity: " + o;
```

ROTATION: 0
OPACITY: 100

We've created two variables, r and o, which define the rotation value and the opacity value of the Text layer, respectively. We then use the addition operators to add String values to the variables. In the Source Text property, you can add a String value, but you can also add a String value to another type of value, which will produce a single String value. The String value "\r" produces a text action which is a command to go to the next line, so we now have the result on two different lines.

Now that the Text layer can display the opacity value, we can visualize what's going on. Let's write this in the expression editor of the Opacity property of the Text layer:

```
var x = rotation;

if (x < 90)
{100}
else
{50};
```

ROTATION: 89
OPACITY: 100

ROTATION: 90
OPACITY: 50

How if / else works

if / else are **Keywords** known as **Conditional Statement**.
It's one statement, so again you can fit everything onto one line, like this:

```
var x = rotation;
if (x < 90) {100} else {50};
```

if (condition) {expression 1 or result 1} else {expression 2 or result 2};

You should always remember that Expression works with 4 essential values: **Number, Array, String and Boolean values**. For **if / else** keywords, Expression works by using the last value, the **Boolean**. Remember that a **Boolean value** answers a comparison with **true** or **false**. If you write this in a Source Text property:

```
var x = 30;
x>25;
```

TRUE

The Boolean value verifies a condition:

CASE true

```
var x = 45;
if (x < 90) {100} else {50};
```

Produces: 100

CASE false

```
var x = 95;
if (x < 90) {100} else {50};
```

Produces: 50

A few keywords

var and if / else are some of the expression keywords. The good thing is that there are not that many to know. When reading an expression, it can sometimes feel super complicated, but this is actually a visual trick, or at least a false impression, which mainly comes from the variables. You might often feel that you don't know a certain term, or can't understand a certain expression, since there are words you don't know. This is because variables are named arbitrarily, but they are only variables—you don't need to know their names to understand them. When you take a closer look, you'll see there are really just a few terms you need to know, but the combinations are infinite—that's the Power of Expression!

Expressions are made of:

Values

Operators

Variables

Objects

Keywords

Comments

Expressions

The power
of index

Index number

So far, we've seen how we can select a value within an Array value by using the **Index number**.

```
f = [32,19,42];
f[1];
```

or

```
f = [32,19,42][1];
```

The result will be 19.

ONLY ARRAY VALUES HAVE ZERO-BASED INDEX NUMBERS

The **Index number** is found everywhere, and can help you to very easily locate any object or value. The **Index number** is a **Number value**; just as we can locate a value within an Array value, we can also locate the objects with the **Index number**. **The Index number for an Array is the only one that is zero-based—all of the other Index numbers you'll encounter begin counting from 1.**

◉	►	1	🟩	Green Solid 1
◉	►	2	🟨	Yellow Solid 1
◉	►	3	🟦	Blue Solid 1
◉	►	4	🟥	Red Solid 1
◉	►	5	⬜	White Solid 1

For example, if you want to link the position of the White Solid 1 layer to the Green Solid 1 layer position, you can write in the expression editor of the position property of the White Solid 1:

```
thisComp.layer("Green Solid 1").position;
```

Thanks to the **Index number**, you can define this without having to write the name of the layer:

```
thisComp.layer(1).position;
```

The **Index number** gives the rank of the Object layer, starting from 1 in the hierarchy of the Object composition.

For layer

thisComp.layer(INDEX NUMBER).position;

```
thisComp.layer(1).position; // Will produce the position value of Green Solid 1
thisComp.layer(2).position; // Will produce the position value of Yellow Solid 1
thisComp.layer(3).position; // Will produce the position value of Blue Solid 1
thisComp.layer(4).position; // Will produce the position value of Red Solid 1
thisComp.layer(5).position; // Will produce the position value of White Solid 1
```

We can use a **String value (Name)** or a **Number value (Index Number)** to call an Object layer.

In **thisComp.layer()**, **layer()** is actually a method. You'll remember that a method is an Object inside an Object: Object.method(argument). This method allows us to select which layer we want to call inside the actual composition.

For properties

thisComp.layer(1).transform(INDEX NUMBER)

○	▼ ■ 1	■ Green Solid 1
	▼ Transform	Reset
	○ Anchor Point	540.0 540.0
	○ Position	540.0 540.0
	○ Scale	🔗 100.0 100.0 %
	○ Rotation	0 +0.0°
	○ Opacity	100 %

```
thisComp.layer(1).transform(1); // Will produce the Anchor Point value
thisComp.layer(1).transform(2); // Will produce the Position value
thisComp.layer(1).transform(3); // Will produce the Scale value
thisComp.layer(1).transform(4); // Will produce the Rotation value
thisComp.layer(1).transform(5); // Will produce the Opacity value
```

The **transform()** method only works with a **Number value** and allows us to select which properties of the layer we want to call.

For effect

Effects are objects and **effect()** is the method we use to call an effect within a layer. Just as with a layer, you can call it with its name using a String value as an argument, but you can also use the Index number to locate an effect and the objects it contains.

Let's add some effects to the **Green Solid 1:**

▶ *fx* Gaussian Blur	Reset	About..	
▶ *fx* CC Composite	Reset	About..	
▼ *fx* CC Radial Fast Blur	Reset	About..	
○ Center	⊕ 540.0 540.0		
▶ ○ Amount	50.0		
○ Zoom	Standard ⌄		

Let's say I want to link the anchor point of the White Solid 1 layer to the center property of the CC Radial Fast Blur effect of the Green Solid 1 layer. Let's open the expression editor of the anchor point of the White Solid 1 layer:

```
thisComp.layer("Green Solid 1").effect("CC Radial Fast Blur").param("Center");
```

param("Name") is the method used to call whichever Object property from the effect you want to use. Shortening it by removing **.param()** also works:

```
thisComp.layer("Green Solid 1").effect("CC Radial Fast Blur")("Center");
```

The great thing, as I mentioned before, is that it works exactly like an Object layer so you can use the **Index number** to define the effect. So, it could also be written like this:

```
thisComp.layer("Green Solid 1").effect(3)(1);
```

or to shorten it even more

```
thisComp.layer(1).effect(3)(1);
```

CC Radial Fast Blur is the third effect in the hierarchy, and Center is the first parameter in the hierarchy.

This is very useful when you don't want to write the entire name, or don't have time to do so. **Just make sure it stays in the same order in the hierarchy**. For example, if you remove an Object effect, this will change the value of the **Index number** of the effect; in our example, if I were to remove the CC Composite effect, the CC Radial Fast Blur would have an **Index number** of 2, not 3.

The power of index

The **Index number** really comes into its own when used to duplicate a layer and distribute the copies.

Let's create a Solid layer and make a circle mask in the center, so it looks like this:

Reveal its position property and in the parametric position value give it the coordinates [0,540], then open the expression editor of the position property and write:

```
offset = 150;
[position[0]+offset*index,position[1]];
```

Now duplicate the Solid layer 5 times, and you should have something like this:

We first created a variable, which we named offset. We then assigned it the Number value 150, which determines the spacing that we want between the circles. We then split the initial position coordinates as an Array value, so the circle layers have the same parametric position value, except we added to the x coordinate the offset variable multiplied by the term **index**. The **index** is a value of the Object layer producing a Number value, which is the Index number of the layer in the hierarchy:

| index; | is a simplification of | thisLayer.index; |

Layer **Index number**:	position[0] + offset*index		The great advantage of
Circle 1:	position[0] + 150	*1	this is that you can make
Circle 2:	position[0] + 150	*2	geometrically accurate shapes
Circle 3:	position[0] + 150	*3	with uniform spacing, which can
Circle 4:	position[0] + 150	*4	give a huge boost to your design
Circle 5:	position[0] + 150	*5	or animation.
Circle 6:	position[0] + 150	*6	

Property index

We can use the **Index number** to duplicate and offset layers, the same as can be achieved for properties.

This time, let's create a circle **from a shape layer** at the center of the comp:

		1	★ Shape Layer 1	
	▼ Contents			Add: ○
		▼ Ellipse 1		Normal ⌄
		▼ Ellipse Path 1		
			○ Size	160.0 160.0
			○ Position	0.0 0.0
		► Fill 1		Normal ⌄
		▼ Transform: Ellipse 1		
			○ Anchor Point	0.0 0.0
			○ Position	0.0 0.0
			○ Scale	100.0 100.0 %
			○ Skew	0.0
			○ Skew Axis	0 +0.0 °
			○ Rotation	0 +0.0 °
			○ Opacity	100 %
	▼ Transform			Reset
			○ Anchor Point	0.0 0.0
			○ Position	540.0 540.0
			○ Scale	100.0 100.0 %
			○ Rotation	0 +0.0 °
			○ Opacity	100 %

The great thing about shape layers is that you can have multiple shapes on one single layer. This is essentially like having a composition with multiple layers, although it works differently to a regular layer when it comes to using the **Index number** on a shape. A shape is an Object like everything else you'll find in the hierarchy of an Object layer, it just doesn't have a direct index value to see its position in the hierarchy; fortunately, there's another way for us to know this.

Let's change the parametric position values of the Ellipse Path 1 to 300 on x and 0 on y.

⊙	▼ ■ 1	★ Shape Layer 1	
	▼ Contents		Add: ●
⊙	▼ Ellipse 1	Normal ⌄	
⊙	▼ Ellipse Path 1	▤ ▤	
	Ò Size	∞ 160.0 160.0	
	Ò Position	300.0 0.0	
⊙	► Fill 1	Normal ⌄	
	▼ Transform: Ellipse 1		
	Ò Anchor Point	0.0 0.0	
	Ò Position	0.0 0.0	
	Ò Scale	∞ 100.0 100.0 %	
	Ò Skew	0.0	
	Ò Skew Axis	0 +0.0°	
	Ò Rotation	0 +0.0°	
	Ò Opacity	100 %	

In the rotation property of the Ellipse 1, open the expression editor and write this:

```
t = thisProperty.propertyGroup(2).propertyIndex;
value + t * 60;
```

Now duplicate the Ellipse 1 group five times:

⊙	▼ ■ 1	★ Shape Layer 1	
	▼ Contents		Add: ●
⊙	► Ellipse 6	Normal ⌄	
⊙	► Ellipse 5	Normal ⌄	
⊙	► Ellipse 4	Normal ⌄	
⊙	► Ellipse 3	Normal ⌄	
⊙	► Ellipse 2	Normal ⌄	
⊙	► Ellipse 1	Normal ⌄	

The result should be this:

```
t = thisProperty.propertyGroup(2).propertyIndex;

value + t * 60;
```

thisProperty

thisProperty is a term used to call the property where the expression lives; remember, a property in After Effects is an Object in Expression, and it works like **thisComp** or **thisLayer**. In our example, we are writing an expression in the rotation property of Ellipse 1, so when we write **thisProperty** we're calling the rotation object of Ellipse 1.

propertyGroup()

propertyGroup() works by reversing the hierarchy, starting from the smallest to the biggest group - this is a method that will produce the group container of the property.

Just as we've done before, we'll use a Text layer to verify what we're doing, so let's add a Text Layer and write this in the Source Text property:

```
r = thisComp.layer("Shape Layer 1").content("Ellipse 1").transform.rotation;
groupNumber = 1;


r.propertyGroup(groupNumber).name;
```

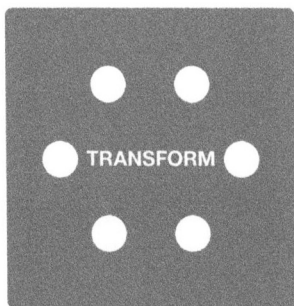

First, we created a variable that we named r, and assigned to it the rotation object of the Ellipse 1. We then created a second variable named groupNumber, and assigned it the Number value 1. Finally, we called the variable r, which is the rotation property and used the **propertyGroup()** method, with an argument—the groupNumber variable. This method produces the first group container of the property, which is an Object, and an Object can be defined by its name, so adding the **name** value to the Object will produce the name of the group: Transform.

propertyIndex

As we've just seen, the expression produces the String value Transform, which is the name of the first group within the hierarchy where the rotation property of Ellipse 1 is located. Now, to make sure what I described is correct, let's add this to the expression of the Text layer:

```
r = thisComp.layer("Shape Layer 1").content("Ellipse 1").transform.rotation;
groupNumber = 1;

groupName = r.propertyGroup(groupNumber).name;
groupIndex = r.propertyGroup(groupNumber).propertyIndex;

groupName + "\r" + groupIndex;
```

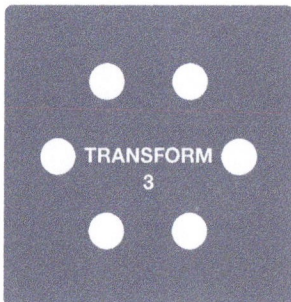

The first line produces the name of the group, Transform, while the second produces the Index number of the group in the hierarchy of the Ellipse 1: 3. Transform is the third group In Ellipse 1, after the Ellipse Path 1 and Fill 1 groups.

		1	★ Shape Layer 1		
O		▼ Contents		Add: O	
O		► Ellipse 6	Normal	∨	
O		► Ellipse 5	Normal	∨	
O		► Ellipse 4	Normal	∨	
O		► Ellipse 3	Normal	∨	
O		► Ellipse 2	Normal	∨	
O		▼ Ellipse 1	Normal	∨	
O		► Ellipse Path 1			
O		► Fill 1	Normal	∨	
		▼ Transform: Ellipse 1			
		Ö Anchor Point	0.0 0.0		
		Ö Position	0.0 0.0		
		Ö Scale	100.0 100.0%		
		Ö Skew	0.0		
		Ö Skew Axis	0 +0.0		
		Ö Rotation	1x +0.0		
		Ö Opacity	100%		

Now we want to move to the next level by selecting the higher group in the hierarchy, which is Ellipse 1. Let's just change the Number value of the variable groupNumber from 1 to 2 and see what it produces:

```
r = thisComp.layer("Shape Layer 1").content("Ellipse 1").transform.rotation;
groupNumber = 2;

groupName = r.propertyGroup(groupNumber).name;
groupIndex = r.propertyGroup(groupNumber).propertyIndex;

groupName + "\r" + groupIndex;
```

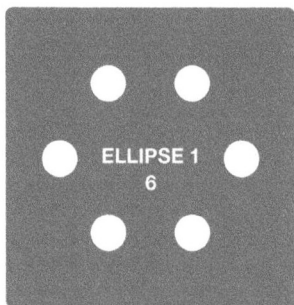

ELLIPSE 1
6

We can see that when we increase the Number value in the **propertyGroup()** method, it moves higher in the hierarchy. Ellipse 1 is the group container of the Transform group and is located in the sixth position within the list of Ellipse groups.

👁	▼ ■ 1 ★ Shape Layer 1		
	▼ Contents		Add: ❍
👁	► Ellipse 6	Normal	⌄
👁	► Ellipse 5	Normal	⌄
👁	► Ellipse 4	Normal	⌄
👁	► Ellipse 3	Normal	⌄
👁	► Ellipse 2	Normal	⌄
👁	► Ellipse 1	Normal	⌄

Remember, groups are just Objects, despite the fact we're calling them groups in this chapter. If I changed the value of the groupNumber to 3, it would move to an even higher group:

```
r = thisComp.layer("Shape Layer 1").content("Ellipse 1").transform.rotation;
groupNumber = 3;

groupName = r.propertyGroup(groupNumber).name;
groupIndex = r.propertyGroup(groupNumber).propertyIndex;

groupName + "\r" + groupIndex;
```

This is confirmed when we check the hierarchy of the layer. Note that Contents is the second group in the hierarchy of the Object layer; Marker is the first group, but it's not shown when you reveal the properties of the layer because it's a hidden group.

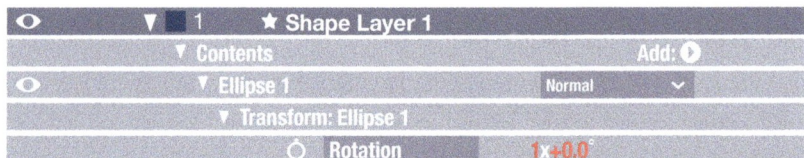

From within one property, we can select any group (or Object) we want to use by using the **propertyGroup()** method. The argument for this method needs to be a Number value—1 is the smallest group, and increasing the value will move up the hierarchy to the larger groups.

propertyGroup(Number value)

propertyIndex produces the Index number of the group in the hierarchy.

Now let's return to our original expression:

```
t = thisProperty.propertyGroup(2).propertyIndex;

value + t * 60;
```

We were able to distribute the copies using the initial value of the Ellipse group by using the term **value**; we then added the Index number of the Ellipse group represented by the variable t, multiplied by 60 so that each Ellipse would be distributed with 60 degrees of space from the others.

You can use the same **propertyGroup()** method for the properties of all the Object effects, and every Object in a layer can be indexed like this. Just keep in mind that **propertyGroup()** works backward, producing the smallest Object containing the Object and then moving incrementally towards the biggest. **propertyIndex** also works for any Object in the hierarchy of a layer. If you call an Object in a layer and add **propertyIndex**, it will produce the index position of the Object within the larger Object container.

Throughout this chapter, we see that Objects can either be called by their name or their Index number.

Insight

Object

Compositions, layers, properties, cameras, lights and effects are all Objects—they contain values, or even other Objects. The best way to understand what an Object is, is to create one.

We've seen how to create an Array value:

```
f = [100,200];
f[0]; // will produce the Number value 100
f[1]; // will produce the Number value 200
f; // will produce the Array value
```

We created the variable f, which we assigned to the Array value; you can create an Object in the same way, and it will behave like a regular Object. Let's create a new Text layer, open the expression editor of the Source Text property and type this:

```
myObject = {value1: [100,100], value2: 45, value3: 38};

myObject.value1; // Will produce 100,100
myObject.value2; // Will produce 45
myObject.value3; // Will produce 38
```

The Object that we just created will only exist in the expression where we created it (you can't call an Object created from another expression). Remember, the general rule is that an expression only exists within itself.

The great thing about knowing this is that it can help you to understand how an Object, such as the position property, exists. Written in an expression, the position property would look like this:

```
Position = {value: [540,540],
name: "Position",
};

Position.value; // will produce 540,540
Position.name; // will produce Position
```

But we also know that Objects can contain other Objects—for example, the position property is inside an Object group called Transform:

```
Transform = {name: "Transform",
Position:{value:[540,540],
name:"Position",
}
};

Transform.name; // will produce Transform
Transform.Position.value; // will produce 540,540
Transform.Position.name; // will produce Position
```

**To create a value in an Object,
you need to pair the value with a name:**

nameValue 1: value 1

To create an Object:

objectName = {
nameValue 1: value 1,
nameValue 2: value 2,
...
nameValue n: value n};

and to call the value:

objectName.nameValue n;

function()

We've seen how to create our own Object, and we've also seen a specific Object: Method. Method can cause an operation on values to produce a new value. But what if the method we need doesn't exist, and we want to create our own? It's time to introduce the keyword **function**:

To create a function:

```
function nameFunction (){
Your Function
return result
};
```

and to call the function:

```
nameFunction();
```

Let's see how this works with an example. Create an Ellipse shape layer and position it on the upper-left corner of the composition:

Let's open the expression editor of the position property of the layer and write:

```
function center (){
return [thisComp.width/2,thisComp.height/2];
};

center();
```

We just created a function to center the layer at the center of the composition.

function nameFunction

To create a function, we first need to write the **function** keyword, then name the function. In our example, we named the function center. **You can name a function whatever you want, just like a variable**, as long as you respect the rules we mentioned on naming a variable. This also applies to any new term you create - don't use a number first, and don't use a term that's already in use within Expression.

()

After naming the function, you need to add parentheses.

{}

We open the curly brackets to define the function. Remember, when we write an expression it can be written entirely between curly brackets; when you create a function, it's like creating an expression that can be called by a shortcut.

return

Inside the curly brackets we can write a function, just as we write an expression that lives on its own. It's important to note that the result of the function needs to be written with the keyword **return**, so it will produce the value created by the function. Without this, it won't produce anything; when Expression reaches **return**, the function will stop executing. **The return keyword is a specific rule for this case, and the result of the function needs to be on the same line for this to work**.
In our example, we only have one statement, so we write the statement directly after the **return** keyword. We'll need an Array value to produce a position value, so in the bracket we'll create an Array value to describe the x and y coordinates. **width** and **height** are values of the composition, which will produce Number values for the width and height of the composition; dividing these by 2, gives us the middle of each dimension.

Call the function

Once you've created and defined the function, you have to call it, just as you call an Object. Creating is not using - when you create an Object or a function in Expression, you still have to call it to use it. To call the function, we type the name of the function that we want to use, but remember that the name followed by **parentheses is what activates the function**. In this case, center() should produce the middle of the width and the middle of the height of the actual composition, which is the exact location of the center of the composition.

We've created a function that can work by itself, but let's say we wanted to manipulate some values:

> **To create a function with arguments:**
>
> function nameFunction (arguments){
> Your Function with arguments
> return result
> };
>
> **and to call the function with arguments:**
>
> nameFunction(arguments);

Let's try to create a function where we invert the x and y coordinates of the Shape layer, while still in the expression editor of the position property:

Using 1 argument

```
function invert (a){
return [a[1],a[0]];
};

invert(position);
```

or

Or using 2 arguments

```
function invert (a,b){
return [b,a];
};

invert(position[0],position[1]);
```

First, when we move the layer around or change the parametric position values, you can see that it's working; second, you'll notice that we can use either one or several arguments inside the parentheses, we just need to make sure they are separated by a comma.

> **nameFunction (argument 1, argument 2,..., argument n)**

Now, let's remove the expression and give the Shape layer negative coordinates, let's say -500 on x and -1000 on y.

We can see that the Shape layer is now outside of the composition but we want it to be inside, so let's write a function in the expression editor of the position property:

```
function positive (a){
return [Math.abs(a[0]),Math.abs(a[1])];
};

positive(position);
```

This time we use the **Math.abs()** method, which always produces a positive Number value. For any Number value entered as the argument, a negative value will be turned into a positive and a positive value will produce the same positive value. This function ensures that the coordinates of the position will always be positive - in our case -500 pixels on x and -1000 pixels on y will be turned into 500 and 1000. But what about if we make the position values -4000 on x and -4000 on y? Again, the Shape layer will disappear from our composition, and the function will produce [4000,4000]. Let's add another method to our function.

```
function positive (a){
return [clamp(Math.abs(a[0]),0,width),clamp(Math.abs(a[1]),0,height)];
};

positive(position);
```

We've added a method called **clamp()**, which works exactly as it sounds:

```
clamp(value, minimum value, maximum value);
```

This method produces the result of the value input clamped between a minimum and a maximum Number value. In our case, we want to make sure it's inside the composition, so we clamp the x position between 0 and the **width** value of the composition, and the y position between 0 and the **height** value of the composition; in this way, whatever value we enter it will always be inside the composition.

We can see that we have one last thing to fix, because the Anchor Point is in the center of the circle, so when the parametric values are above the maximum values, ¾ of the circle disappears. We want to make sure the circle is always entirely in the composition; to do this, we'll use the value of the Size property in the Ellipse Path.

○	▼ ▬ 1	★ Shape Layer 1		
	▼ Contents		Add: ◐	
○	▼ Ellipse 1		Normal	∨
○	▼ Ellipse Path 1		▦ ▧	
	Ò Size		∾ 160.0 160.0	
	Ò Position		0.0 0.0	
○	► Fill 1		Normal	∨
	► Transform: Ellipse			
	▼ Transform		Reset	
	Ò Anchor Point		0.0 0.0	
	Ò Position		1080.0 1080.0	
	Ò Scale		∾ 100.0 100.0 %	
	Ò Rotation		0 +0.0	
	Ò Opacity		100 %	

Let's edit the expression in the position property:

```
function positive (a){
size = content("Ellipse 1").content("Ellipse Path 1").size;
return [clamp(Math.abs(a[0]),size[0]/2,width-size[0]/2),
clamp(Math.abs(a[1]),size[1]/2,height-size[1]/2)];
};

positive(position);
```

works even whe
you increase th
Size of the Ellip
path

Method

Why did we do all of that? Look closely—function(arguments), does this remind you of anything?

Math.round(Number value)

Object.method(arguments)

function(arguments)

Object.method(arguments)

function(arguments)

Yes, it's exactly that—**a method is a function. A function is an Object and a method is a function nested within an Object**. So, if you're able to make your own function, you definitely understand how a method works. In the same way as we understood what an Object was by creating one, we can see more clearly what a method is by creating our own.

function() or object.method()

We've already encountered methods like **Math.round()**, **Math.Abs()**, etc.
These really look like functions as part of an Object. Let's reuse the center
function we created earlier in this chapter and build it within an Object:

```
essential = {center: function (){
return [thisComp.width/2,thisComp.height/2];
}};

essential.center();
```

We created an Object essential that contains the function center we created earlier,
you'll notice that an Object can contain values as well as methods.

You can even add a function to an Object that already exists:

```
transform.center = function (){
return [thisComp.width/2,thisComp.height/2];
};

transform.center();
```

This is also the case when adding values:

```
essential = {}; // Create new object

essential.value1 = "value"// Add a new value

essential.value1; // Call the value
```

this

By this point, you'll be aware that composition, layer, camera, light, effect, property and method are all built-in Objects, which means they're created within the software and accessible directly inside the realm of Expression by calling their corresponding terms, without the need to define them. We also have terms that make calling these Objects even faster.

Let's say we have a square Shape layer in a composition:

Let's open the expression editor of its rotation property:

```
thisProperty.add10 = function(){
return thisProperty + 10;
};


thisProperty.add10();
```

or

```
thisProperty.add10 = function(){
return this + 10;
};


thisProperty.add10();
```

You'll see that if you apply this expression to any of the other properties it will still work, adding the Number value 10 to any property. Using the Objects **thisComp**, **thisLayer**, **thisProperty** or even **this** enables you to call an Object that is not yet defined within a function. **this** can be described as a shortcut, and it will take the same form as the Object container.

Now that we've gone into the details of how to create your own Objects, it should be easier for you to understand and manipulate them.

Length

Distance

The **length()** method calculates the distance between two layers. In our goal to harmonize your daily workflow, to simplify interactions and changes, this method will be fundamental for its simplicity.

First, let's see exactly what we mean by the distance between two layers. We'll be working in a 2D environment, but all of the following examples can also be used in a 3D environment.

Let's create two circle Shape layers, then place one at [200,540] and the other at [900,540] within the composition. On top of these, let's add a Text layer that we'll use to display the information:

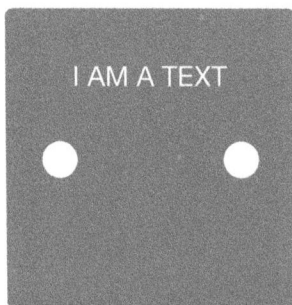

Vector

Now, we need to calculate the distance between the two Shape layers. How can we do this? By using math and vectors - the position value of a layer is a vector, and a vector is composed of two coordinates that give the direction on X and Y.

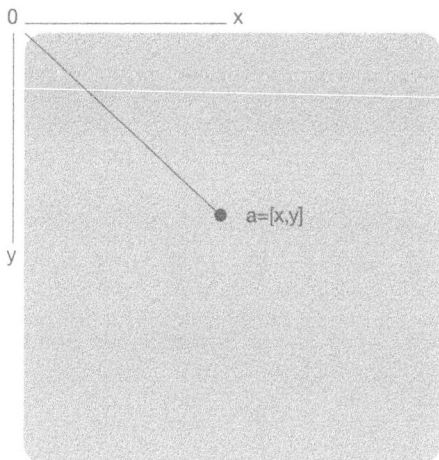

0 _____ x

a=[x,y]

y

Representing
a vector in a
composition

The mathematical formula for calculating the length of a vector is from the origin [0,0] to its position:

origin= [0,0]
a= [x,y]

$$Length= \sqrt{(x-0)^2+ (y-0)^2}$$

So to calculate the length between two vectors it should look like this:

a= [x,y]
b= [x2,y2]

$$Length= \sqrt{(x2-x)^2+ (y2-y)^2}$$

This looks like something we can do in Expression because the position value has the X and Y values in the Array value so for the circle Shape layers - it would look like this:

Shape layer 1= [200,540]
Shape layer 2= [900,540]

$$Length= \sqrt{(900-200)^2+ (540-540)^2}$$

Let's convert this mathematical formula into the language of Expression. As usual, we'd like to display the result in the Text layer, so let's reveal the Source Text property and type this into the expression editor:

```
layer1 = thisComp.layer('Shape Layer 1').position;
layer2 = thisComp.layer('Shape Layer 2').position;

Math.sqrt(Math.pow((layer2[0]-layer1[0]),2)+Math.pow((layer2[1]-layer1[1]),2));
```

This is the exact distance between these two layers. Now, let's take a closer look at what we used in the expression:

We created two variables, layer1 and layer2, which stock the position values of the circle Shape layers, from where we can select the x position and y position with their respective Index numbers [0] and [1]. **Math.sqrt(Number value)** is the method to calculate a square root and **Math.pow(Number value,exponent)** calculates the power of a number; these are perfect, because we want to calculate the square of these subtractions.

Now when we move the circle Shape layers around, the distance will be updated.

To begin with, what information would we need to make this animation? The icons change size when the cursor is getting closer, so if we could know the distance between the cursor and the icons, we could write an expression on the scale property of the icons that modifies their size depending on how close the cursor is.

Let's import a picture of a cursor into the composition (or you can of course create your own), then rename the layer "CURSOR". Next, let's create a square Shape layer that we'll name "LEADER"; you can make its size 60×60 and position it at 160 on x and 1000 on y.

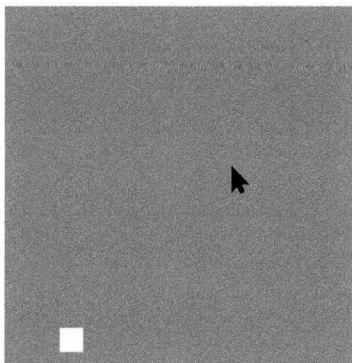

The square Shape layer will need to grow from the bottom, just like in the Dock bar, so let's move the anchor point to the bottom of the layer. Actually, let's move it to the bottom left corner—you'll see why later on:

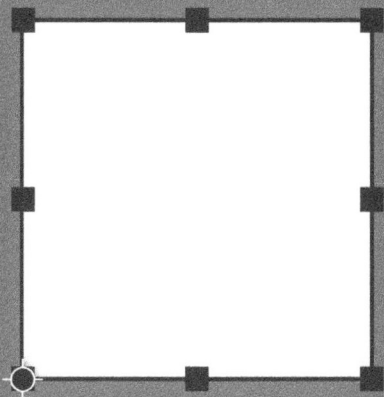

Now as we said, the purpose of this animation is to have the icons grow bigger when the cursor moves closer, so we probably have to play with the scale property of the square Shape layer. Let's open the expression editor of the scale property and type this:

```
cursor = thisComp.layer('CURSOR').position;
x = length (position,cursor);

linear (x,0,300,[200,200],[100,100]);
```

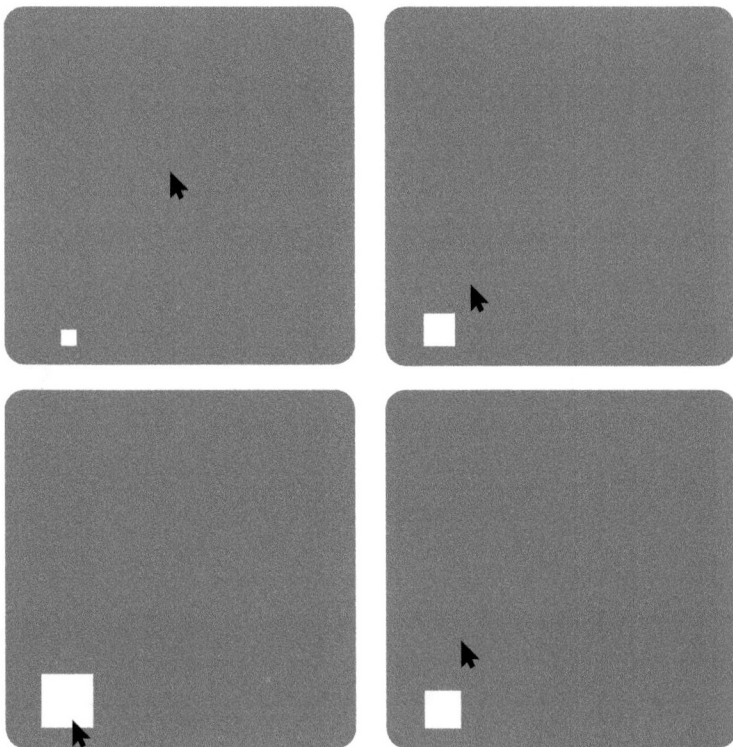

So, the icon will grow bigger when the cursor is closer, then get smaller when we move away, behaving just how we wanted.

Interpolation methods

The **linear()** method is also super useful. This is an interpolation method that works like a converter, and can convert one value from a range of values to an equivalent value in a different range of values. In our example, the problem we have is that the distance between the layers produces a Number value, while the scale property has an Array value composed of two values [width,height]. Essentially, it works like the Rule of Three, and you'll need 5 arguments for this method:

linear(Value,Minimum Input,Maximum Input,Minimum Output,Maximum Output)

If you only enter 3 arguments, it will by default use the minimum and maximum Input range from 0 to 1:

linear(Value,Minimum Output,Maximum Output)

is the same as:

linear(Value,0,1,Minimum Output, Maximum Output)

Like the keyframe interpolation mode, you have the linear, ease, ease in and ease out modes, which work in exactly the same way as the **linear()** method:

linear() ease() easeIn() easeOut()

Type this in the Source Text property of a Text layer:

```
x = 0;
linear(x,0,1,[0,0],[1000,1000]);
// will produce 0,0
```

```
x = 0.35;
linear(x,0,1,[0,0],[1000,1000]);
// will produce 350,350
```

```
x = 0.5;
linear(x,0,1,[0,0],[1000,1000]);
// will produce 500,500
```

```
x = 1;
linear(x,0,1,[0,0],[1000,1000]);
// will produce 1000,1000
```

Looking back at our example, we created a variable named cursor, to which we assigned the position value of the cursor layer. With the **length()** method, we calculated the distance between the cursor position value and the icon position value, entering both of these values as arguments; next we assign the distance to a variable named x. We then used a **linear()** method.

```
linear(x,0,300,[200,200],[100,100])
```

When the distance x is at zero, it will produce a value of [200,200], and when the distance is at 300 it will produce a value of [100,100]. This is because it's an interpolation method, so all the values between 0 and 300 will be converted into a value between [200,200] and [100,100]. So, when the distance is closer it gets bigger, and when it's further away it gets smaller.

One layer to control them all

Now we want to have multiple icons on the Dock bar. One of the goals of using Expression is to be able to find harmony and balance in our animation—we're trying to create an interactive behavior without using too many keyframes, but also without too many expressions.

Let's duplicate the square Shape layer named "LEADER" and rename the new square Shape layer to "FOLLOWER":

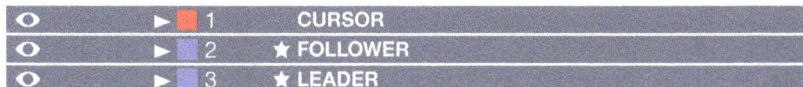

○	► ■ 1	CURSOR
○	► ■ 2	★ FOLLOWER
○	► ■ 3	★ LEADER

Make sure that the FOLLOWER layer is above the LEADER layer in the hierarchy, as this will be important later on.

The FOLLOWER layer now works like a clone of the LEADER layer—it has the same position value and expression on the scale property. Let's see what happens when I duplicate the FOLLOWER layer a couple of times and offset their positions manually:

This doesn't look right: we don't want them to overlap when it grows, we want to always have the same amount of space between the icons.

thisComp.layer(thisLayer,numberLayer)

Because we want to keep the same amount of space between the layers as they grow so they don't overlap, we need to link the position property of the FOLLOWER layer to the LEADER layer. To do this, let's reveal the position property of the FOLLOWER layer and write in the expression editor:

```
layerBelow = thisComp.layer(thisLayer,1);
[layerBelow.position[0]+ layerBelow.scale[0]*0.7, layerBelow.position[1]];
```

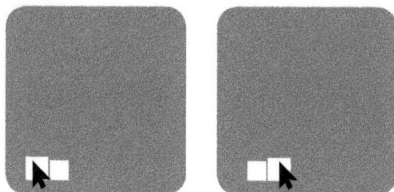

thisComp.layer(thisLayer,numberLayer)

if numberLayer = -2, it calls the second layer above of thisLayer
if numberLayer = -1, it calls the layer above of thisLayer
if numberLayer = 0, it's thisLayer
if numberLayer = 1, it calls the layer below thisLayer
if numberLayer = 2, it calls the second layer below thisLayer
Etc.

We've seen how we can call an Object layer using either its name or its Index number, and this technique also works like the Index number. Essentially, what we are trying to do is take information from the Object layer that is the layer below in the hierarchy to produce the information that we need to apply to the position property of the layer above—like a cascade, but in reverse. In this way, the layer below will control the position of the one above.

So, we have assigned the Object layer that is below in the hierarchy to the variable layerBelow. In the expression, the y position will stay the same, we'll only change the x position. To do this we used the x position of the layer below—calling layerBelow.position[0]—then used an addition operator to add the width scale property of the layer below, which will be multiplied by 0.7. layerBelow.scale[0]*0.7: this will be the space between the layers. I could also have chosen to multiply it by any number—this just determines how much space we want between the icons. The important thing to remember is to multiply it by the width scale property of the layer below, which means that when the layer below is bigger the position of the layer above is further away, and when it is smaller the position will be closer; this way, we can keep the right amount of space between the icons.

thisComp.layer(thisLayer,numberLayer): The great advantage of using this cascade technique is that I will be able to duplicate the FOLLOWER layer to make as many icons as I want, and these layers will already be linked and correctly positioned relative to the layer below:

We should now have our desired result - if you hover the cursor over the icons, they should magnify.

O	►	1		CURSOR
O	►	2	★	FOLLOWER 9
O	►	3	★	FOLLOWER 8
O	►	4	★	FOLLOWER 7
O	►	5	★	FOLLOWER 6
O	►	6	★	FOLLOWER 5
O	►	7	★	FOLLOWER 4
O	►	8	★	FOLLOWER 3
O	►	9	★	FOLLOWER 2
O	►	10	★	FOLLOWER
O	►	11	★	LEADER

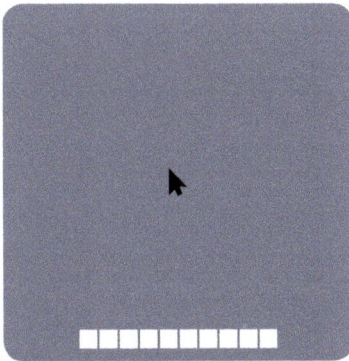

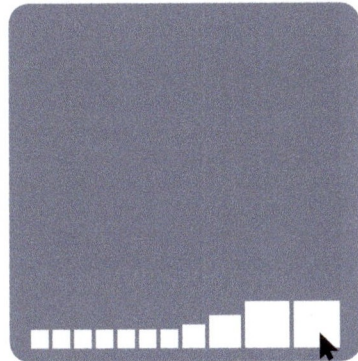

The **length()** method is a very easy way to obtain fantastic, realistic results without too much work. It also connects the elements together, so it's a big help in our quest to find harmony in the project, as everything feels smoother when it's connected.

Time

Generate animation using time

time is an essential value in Expression. It produces a Number value of the current time of the composition in seconds. In a new composition, create a Text layer and in the Source Text property, open the expression editor:

```
time;
```

0	0.50050050050005	1.46813480146813

time is not the timecode of the composition (to verify this, go into the composition settings and change the Start Timecode to 0:01:12:00 - you'll notice that the time hasn't changed). **time** generates the Number value of the current time in the timeline starting from 0. Because we aim to create animations in After Effects, being able to generate a continuous Number value can give us a huge advantage in making animations quickly, and one great benefit that **time** offers is constant frequency.

Let's round off the time number in the Source Text property using the **Math.round()** method to make it easier to read:

```
Math.round(time);
```

0	1	2

Now, let's open the expression editor of the rotation property of the Text layer and write:

```
time*30;
```

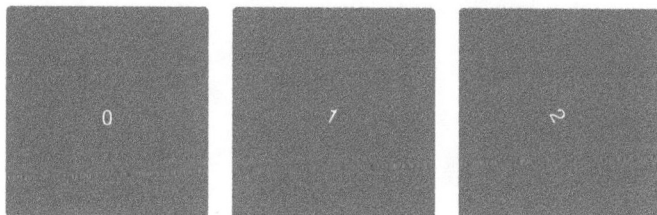

As you can see, the Text layer will rotate according to the time multiplied by 30 to make it faster, so with every second that passes the layer will perform a 30 degree rotation, and will keep rotating at the same frequency through time.

Let's remove that expression from the rotation property. Now let's reveal the scale property of the Text layer and write this in the expression editor:

```
[value[0]*time,value[1]*time];
```

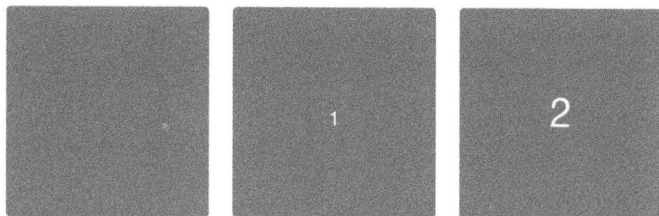

As you can see, the scale of the Text layer grows as time passes. We could have simplified this expression, because we can directly multiply an Array value by a Number value. This works in a similar way as the distributivity within parentheses when you do multiplication: $(x+y)*z = x*z + y*z$

```
[value[0]*time,value[1]*time];
```

is the same as

```
value*time;
```

```
f = [1,2,3];
f*10; // it will produce 10,20,30
```

time produces a Number value that can be directly used in expressions.

inPoint

We've seen that when written by itself, **time** is a value that produces the current time of the composition starting from 0. But it can also be used like the Index number or **name** value, providing us with information about the time of an event.

Create a circle Shape layer and position it in the upper-left corner of the composition:

Now let's give it some life on the timeline—go to the position property and add a keyframe at 1 sec, then move the circle to the right to have a second keyframe at 2 sec. The layer should begin at 0.5 sec and finish at 3 sec. Finally, add a marker to the layer at 1.5 sec and another at 2.5 sec.

Now, as usual let's add a Text layer and open the expression editor of the Source Text property:

thisComp.layer('Shape Layer 1').inPoint;

0.5

As you can see, the **inPoint** value produces a Number value of the time (in seconds) where the circle Shape layer begins.

outPoint

```
thisComp.layer('Shape Layer 1').outPoint;
```

3

outPoint produces a Number value of the time (in seconds) where the Shape layer ends.

If you subtract the **inPoint** value from the **outPoint** value, you will have the duration of the layer in seconds.

```
var start, end;
start = thisComp.layer('Shape Layer 1').inPoint;
end = thisComp.layer('Shape Layer 1').outPoint;
end - start;
```

2.5

You can see on the expression that I created the variables differently. It will work just the same if you create the variables first then assign them later on, it's just another way of writing it; just remember that it won't work if you create the variables without using the keyword **var**:

```
var a, b, c;
a = 10;
b = 10;
c = a + b; // will produce 20
```

Duration

If you want the duration of the composition in seconds, there is a value that works with the Object composition—**duration**.

```
thisComp.duration;
```

10

My composition lasts 10 seconds, so it produces the right number. Note that this value does not exist for an Object layer.

marker

Now, let's see what other time information we can access from the circle Shape layer. Let's display the time of the first marker of the circle Shape layer, so in the Source Text property let's type this:

```
thisComp.layer('Shape Layer 1').marker.key(1).time;
```

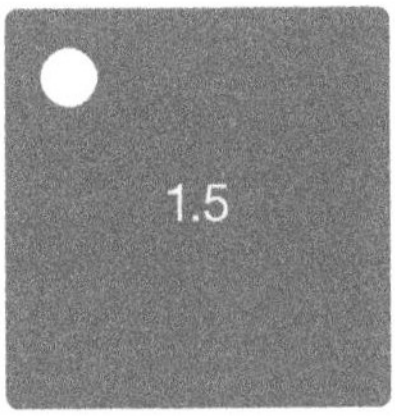

1.5

We can see that when we call the Object Shape layer, we can select its markers with **marker** which is an Object. We then need to use the **key()** method, which defines the marker you want to select. As an argument, you'll need to enter which marker you want to access. This works like an Index number - the first marker is number 1, the second is number 2, etc. We then need to call the **time** value, which will produce a Number value in seconds where the marker is located.

```
thisComp.layer('Shape Layer 1').marker.key(2).time;
```

2.5

As you can see, we're able to show the time of the markers, information that can be used to our great advantage; for example, you can use the marker as a keyframe for animations. First, let's write a new expression in the Source Text property of the Text layer:

```
opacity;
```

The Text layer now displays the Number value of its opacity, which is 100. Now, reveal the opacity property of the Text layer, and let's write an expression:

```
startOpacity = thisComp.layer('Shape Layer 1').marker.key(1).time;
endOpacity = thisComp.layer('Shape Layer 1').marker.key(2).time;

linear (time,startOpacity,endOpacity,10,100);
```

We created a first variable startOpacity, to which we assigned the **time** value of marker 1, and a second variable endOpacity, to which we assigned the **time** value of marker 2. We then used a **linear()** interpolation method, in which we entered **time** as the value argument. This converts the range of **time** values of the markers between 1.5 sec and 2.5 sec into a new range of values that we defined as between 10 and 100, so when the **time** is 1.5 sec or less it will produce 10 in the opacity property, and when it's 2.5 sec or more it will produce 100. Essentially, we used the markers like keyframes—if you move a marker to a different location on the timeline, you'll notice that the animation of the opacity of the Text layer is automatically updated.

Keyframe

Just as we can access the **time** value of a marker, we can also access the **time** value of a keyframe. Let's remove the expression in the opacity property of the Text layer. Now we want to display the time of the first position keyframe of the circle Shape layer, so let's write this in the Source Text property of the Text layer:

thisComp.layer('Shape Layer 1').position.key(1).time;

1

thisComp.layer('Shape Layer 1').position.key(2).time;

2

The first position keyframe of the circle Shape layer is at 1 sec and the second is at 2 sec, so it looks like it's working. If we take a closer look at the expression, we'll see that it works almost like the **marker** Object, except we need to define the Object property where we want to access the keyframes, in our case the **position** Object. To select the keyframe we need the **key()** method, and we then have to add the **time** value to have access to the value.

We can now see that we have access to the time information of the keyframes using the **time** value. You can also use another term from the **key()** method, **value**, which will produce the value of the keyframe called.

thisComp.layer('Shape Layer 1').position.key(1).value;

300,335

thisComp.layer('Shape Layer 1').position.key(2).value;

790,335

nearestKey()

The **key()** method can be replaced with the **nearestKey()** method if you want to produce the value of the closest keyframe at the current time.

```
thisComp.layer('Shape Layer 1').position.nearestKey(time).time;
```

You'll notice that the value changes over time - that's because we entered the **time** value as an argument in the **nearestKey()** method. **time** describes the current time, so it produces Number values at a constant frequency: 0 sec, 1 sec, 2 sec, 3sec etc. This method will thus produce the time of the keyframe that is closest to the current time. However, if you enter a Number value as the argument it will look for the keyframe nearest to this number:

```
thisComp.layer('Shape Layer 1').position.nearestKey(3).time;
```

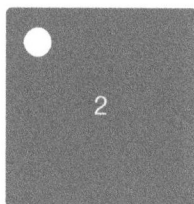

This expression looks for which keyframe is the closest to second 3 and produces its time - it produces 2, which is where the closest keyframe is.

The **nearestKey()** method also works for the marker Object.

```
thisComp.layer('Shape Layer 1').marker.nearestKey(time).time;
```

This expression should produce a Number value, which is the time of the closest marker at the current time.

See values behind shapes

We've seen that we can use **time** as a means of generating a Number value, to create an animation without keyframes, or to access time information on the timeline. Some methods also use the **time** value to initiate other useful tasks.

The **Math.cos()** and **Math.sin()** methods allow us to calculate the Cosine and Sine of an angle in radians, respectively.

a Cosine curve   a Sine curve

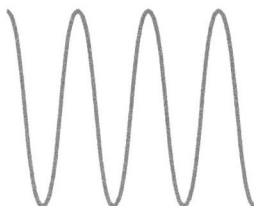

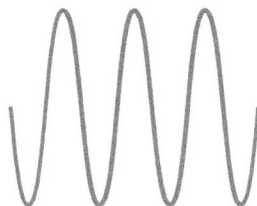

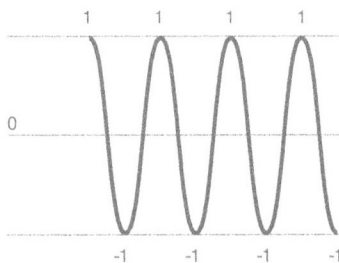

These look pretty similar and rather abstract. In general, Math can be abstract if you don't find real-world uses for it, like with the Cosine and Sine graph phenomena, but once you see how they can be used, everything becomes clearer. I would like you to see them not as shapes, but as values:

a Cosine curve   a Sine curve

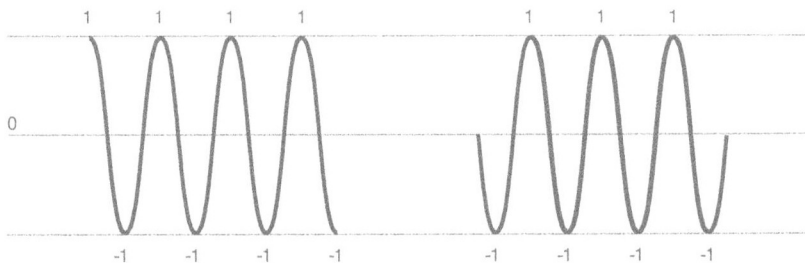

We can see through these graphs, that Cosine and Sine generate values between -1 and 1 at a regular frequency; these can be truly amazing tools that we can use to make animations. The only difference between them is that Cosine starts by producing a value of 1 at 0 sec and Sine starts by producing a value 0 at 0 sec.

Math.cos() and Math.sin()

So how can we generate this type of cycle values in Expression? Again, the **time** value will be rather useful here. If we create a new circle Shape layer, I'll show you that working with Math and Expression is useful not only to generate easy movements, but also to make geometrical shapes, which is exactly what we need for our goal of achieving harmony in our animation.

We've seen that the Cosine and Sine formulas can generate Number values between -1 and 1 over repetitive periods. To use these formulas, we need to enter an argument that can produce all the numbers within a formula, and the only term we know that can generate all the Number values across time is the **time** value. Let's see what happens when we use a **Math.sin()** method on the y axis position of the circle Shape layer. Reveal the position property of the Shape layer and write this in the expression editor:

```
x = thisComp.width/2;
y = thisComp.height/2;

[x,y+Math.sin(time)];
```

We first created two variables, x and y, then assigned them the middle position of each dimension so the layer starts from the center of the comp. The x position doesn't change, but we added the **Math.sin()** method to the y position. We then entered **time** as an argument in the method; however, we cannot see any changes because the movement is too subtle. The method actually produces Number values from -1 to 1, so on the y axis it moves from y-1 to y+1 on the sinusoidal frequencies; our comp is 1080 in height, so the circle should move between 539 and 541. Let's multiply the method by a Number value so we can see something visible.

```
x = thisComp.width/2;
y = thisComp.height/2;

[x,y+Math.sin(time)*400];
```

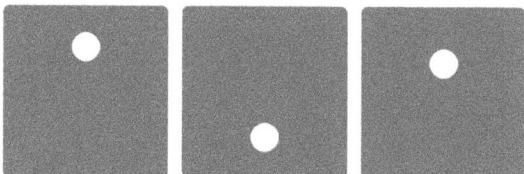

As we can see, the Shape layer goes up and down with a higher amplitude. Now let's do the same with the x axis position of the circle Shape layer using the **Math.cos()** method.

```
x = thisComp.width/2;
y = thisComp.height/2;

[x+Math.cos(time)*400,y+Math.sin(time)*400];
```

To clearly see what's happening, let's look at this through values: both **Math.cos()** and **Math.sin()** produce cycles of Number values between -1 and 1, and we multiplied both of these by 400, so from the center of the composition, we are going to have cycles of Number values going from -400 to +400 on both axes. While **Math.cos()** starts by producing a Number value 1 (which gives us +400 on x), **Math.sin()** begins by producing a Number value 0 (so we have +0 on y).

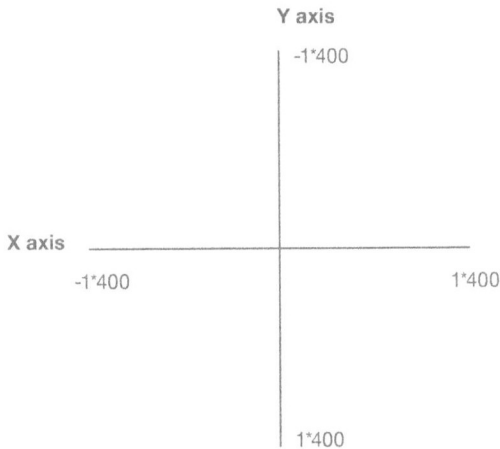

Y axis
-1*400

X axis
-1*400   1*400

1*400

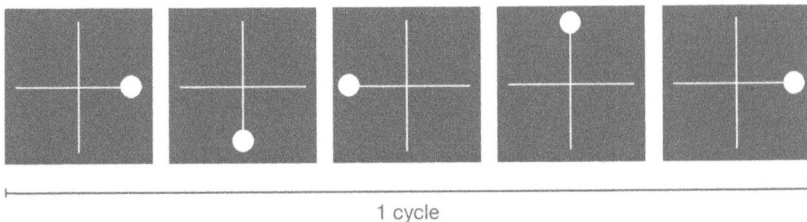

1 cycle

Math.cos() and **Math.sin()** combined gives us a really interesting shape, but to make it more interesting let's add a **Write-on effect** to the circle Shape layer, and in the Brush Position property of this effect we'll write:

```
position;
```

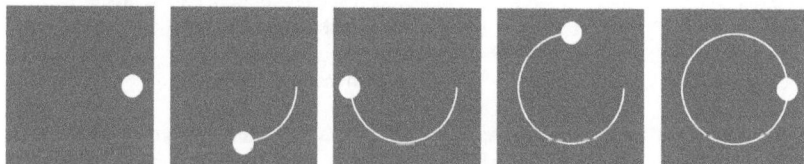

The **Write-on effect** essentially leaves a brush mark behind every movement of the brush position; with the expression we just wrote, the brush position now follows the position of the Shape layer. By doing this, the Write-on effect shows the path of the circle Shape layer. We can see that, thanks to the **Math.cos()** and **Math.sin()**, we were able to make a perfectly circular movement with the circle Shape layer, and it's using **time** as an argument that allows us to use these methods.

To be even clearer within the expression we wrote in the position property of the circle Shape layer, we could have written it this way:

```
x = thisComp.width/2;
y = thisComp.height/2;
radius = 400; // This is the radius of the circle

[x+Math.cos(time)*radius,y+Math.sin(time)*radius];
```

We could have used the **Math.sin()** method on the x axis and the **Math.cos()** method on the y axis, but it's only by combining both of these that we get a full circle. How were we able to visualize this? Remember, focus on the values—**Math.cos()** and **Math.sin()** are both producing values between -1 and 1 at the same regular frequency; they're the same, just delayed.

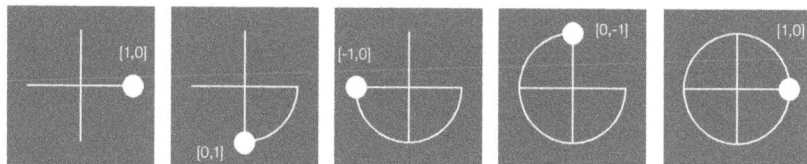

I wanted to show you this because before thinking about the graph, you need to think about how to use it, and which values you'll need or can be produced. When I think of **Math.cos()** or **Math.sin()** methods, I first visualize that they will produce values between -1 and 1 across **time**. Again, expressions are just about values—you can convert them, link them or change them, but in the end you're still just producing values.

valueAtTime()

We can use other methods to take advantage of the **time** value:
valueAtTime() is a method which allows us to access the value of an Object property at the time entered as an argument. What makes this different from calling an Object property's value? The difference is that you can select a specific time of the property, as well as being able to offset this time and control many layers with one single layer. Let's look at a way of spacing the layers out along a path that can be modified.

First, let's create a Null layer and name it "PATH". Let's add three keyframes on its position property: one position [0,540] at 0 sec, the second keyframe at 2 sec, located at the center of the comp [540,540], and the third at 4 sec, at the edge of the comp [1080,540]. It should basically only move on the x axis, so the position path should look like this when you select it:

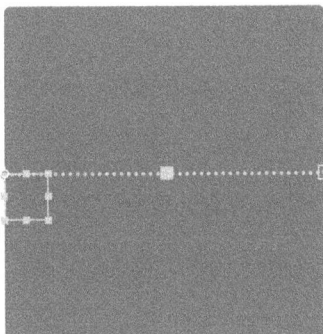

For the middle keyframe, let's turn the spatial interpolation into a Bezier, so we have handles to change the shape of the position path. Try to make it look like this:

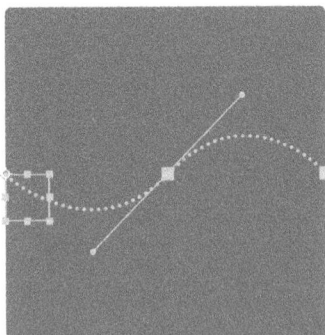

We'll then use this path as a shape to position the layers in the composition. Create a new circle Shape layer, reveal its position property and add a new expression:

```
thisComp.layer('PATH').position.valueAtTime(index-1);
```

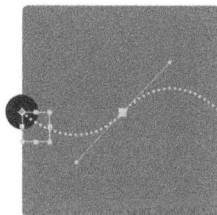

We call the position Object of the PATH layer, and with the **valueAtTime()** method we enter the time of the Object property we want to select as argument. We enter index-1, so the time we set will be based on the Index number of the layer minus 1. Since the circle Shape layer is the first layer in the hierarchy of the composition, it will have the position value of the Path layer at 0 sec.

Because the circle Shape layer has an expression based on the Index number, if we duplicate it, it will offset the next layers and distribute them along this path. To illustrate this, let's duplicate this Circle layer 4 times; the second layer in the hierarchy, 2-1, will be located at 1 sec on the path, and so on:

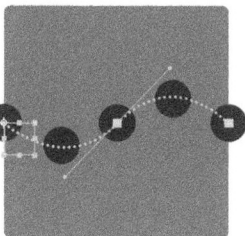

As you can see, the copies of the circle Shape layer now perfectly follow the position of the path we created in the PATH Layer. Now, so that you're aware of the potential of this expression, let's reshape the position of the path and you'll notice that the layers automatically update and follow the new path perfectly:

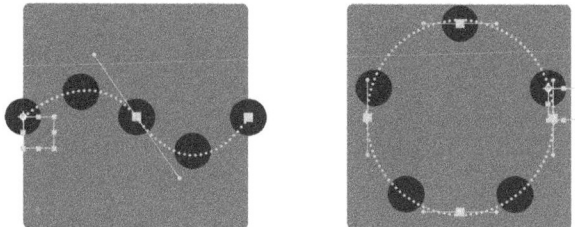

You can see that with this method, we can make perfect shapes or effortlessly align layers along a path, all while maintaining harmony and keeping it easily editable. Also, notice that the **time** value is just a sequence of Number values—you don't need to limit yourself by only using time, you can also selectively control it by using just a part of the time. For example, you can directly enter a Number value like 1, 2, 3 etc., variables, or even an Index number to describe which part of the time you want to use.

speed

The other information we can obtain is speed, for which we have two values: **speed** and **velocity. The speed value produces the speed of the property called per second**. This works exactly like how we measure the speed of a car; for example, if a car were going 60 kilometers in an hour, it would have an average speed of 60 km/h, if it were going at a linear speed. In animation, linear speed, means the speed is the same throughout the animation - for example, if my layer has a keyframe of 50% opacity at 0 second and a keyframe of 100% opacity at 1 second, the property would have increased by 50% in one second, so the speed would have been a linear 50%/s during the animation. But just like driving a car, sometimes you have to go faster or slower, so your speed isn't constant. So, the **speed** value produces a Number value of the speed of the property at the current time. But unlike a car's speed, it can also produce a negative value if the property decreases.

Let's add a circle Shape layer to a composition:

Now let's add some motion to this circle—add two keyframes on the position property of this layer, for example to move it from the left to the right, add a keyframe [340,800] at second 0, and at second 1 let's move it to [800,330]:

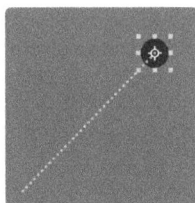

Create a Text layer and in the Source Text property, let's write this in the expression editor:

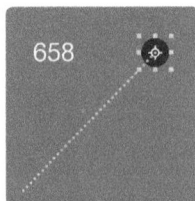

```
Math.round(thisComp.layer('Shape Layer 1').position.speed);
```

We just called the **speed** value from the position property of the circle Shape layer, then used the **Math.round()** method to round out the speed to a whole number. This expression produces the speed of the position property of the layer. As we can see, between 0 sec and 1 sec we have a constant speed, then the speed falls to 0 because the layer is not moving. Now instead of having linear keyframes on the position property, let's change them to Bezier keyframes.

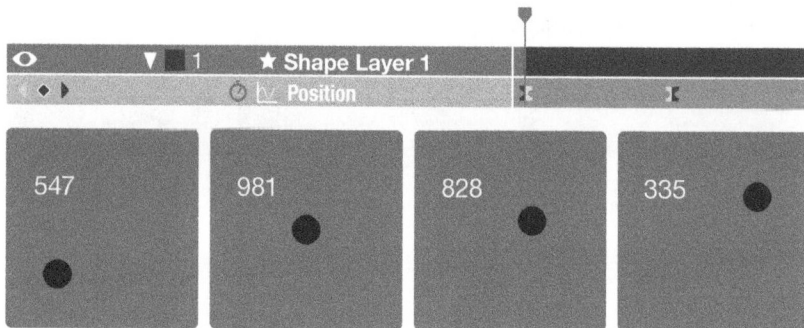

We can see that the speed starts at 0, then increases until the middle position, where it decreases back to 0 at the final position. Now we want the speed to have an impact on the circle Shape layer, so that the faster the circle goes the smaller it is, and the slower it goes the bigger it is. Let's reveal the scale property of the circle Shape layer and write this expression:

```
var s = position.speed/20;
[value[0]-s,value[1]-s];
```

We created a variable, s, to which we assigned the **speed** value of the position Object divided by 20, because as we can see on the Text layer displaying the speed, the speed goes over 1000 but the scale values are only 100, so if we want to keep the layer visible we have to make the **speed** value smaller. The scale value is an Array value made up of two values, width and height, and from each **value** we subtract the variable s. As we can see, the scale property of the layer is now linked to the speed of the position property—when the speed increases, it gets smaller.

velocity

We can also use the **velocity** value. For the position property, this will produce an Array value with two values, the first Number value being the speed of the x position and the second Number value the speed of the y position. Like the speed value, these values can be negative or positive depending on their direction. To see this clearly in our example, let's change the position keyframes back to linear:

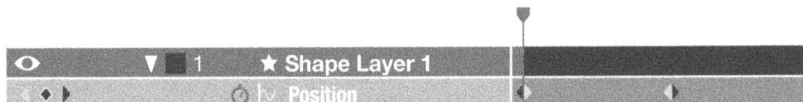

The speed of the layer should now be linear: a constant speed throughout the animation.

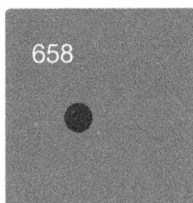

Let's add a new Text layer on the right side of the composition. In the Source Text property of this new Text, we're going to display the **velocity** of the circle Shape layer:

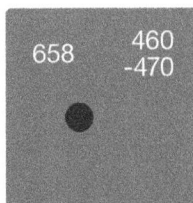

```
t = thisComp.layer('Shape Layer 1').position.velocity;

v1 = Math.round(t[0]);
v2 = Math.round(t[1]);

v1 +"\r"+ v2;
```

We called the **velocity** value from the position Object, which produces an Array value with two Number values. We then we display the first velocity value on one line and the second velocity value on a new line. As we see, it shows that the velocity of the layer is 460 on x and -470 on y, which is exactly the speed of the x and y positions in a 1 second linear animation.

The start position is [340,800] and the final position is [800,330]. If you do the Math for a 1 second linear animation: 800 – 340 for x and 330 – 800 on y we end up with exactly the same result.

speed and **velocity** also work for the other Transform properties, effects properties or properties in general. Using this information to connect properties together, you can bring harmony to your animations.

speedAtTime() and velocityAtTime()

Just as for **value** and **valueAtTime()** method, we have the same complementary methods for the **speed** and **velocity** values.

```
value = valueAtTime(time)
speed = speedAtTime(time)
velocity = velocityAtTime(time)
```

You don't necessary need to use the **time** value as an argument, just like for the **valueAtTime()** method, the argument you enter between the parentheses is the time you want, so you can use the current time or select your own to offset the animation.

Time remapping

Playing with the time in Expression can often help you to quickly create complex animations, as well as making it easier to edit. **You can add expressions to the time remapping property, so do use it**. An animation can be controlled through Time Remapping. Thanks to this, the layers can behave like sliders or buttons in a modern User Interface or HUD design style. Let's see how we can take advantage of this—first, let's create a circle Shape layer with a sharp gradient, like this:

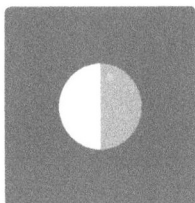

Now we'll animate this circle Shape layer between 0 sec and 1 sec. Let's add two keyframes to the scale property so it grows from 30% at 0 sec to 100% at 1 sec. Let's also make it rotate, so it should go from -90 at 0 sec to 90 at 1 sec.

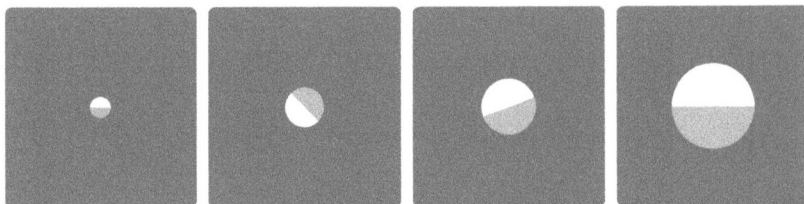

We now have a small animation which lasts 1 sec. Let's pre-compose the circle Shape layer, which should by default create a new composition called Shape Layer 1 Comp 1, which contains our small animation.

In a new composition, create a round rectangle Shape layer in the middle of the composition, make it [800,25] in size.

Let's create a circle Shape layer in the middle of the rectangle Shape layer, and parent it to the rectangle Shape layer.

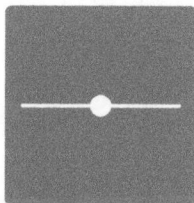

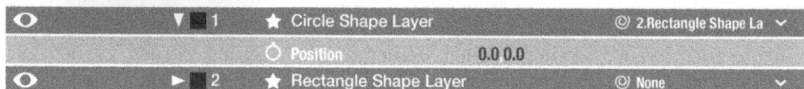

○		▼ ■ 1	★ Circle Shape Layer		◎ 2.Rectangle Shape La ∨
		○ Position		0.0 0.0	
○		► ■ 2	★ Rectangle Shape Layer		◎ None ∨

Since the circle Shape layer is now parented to the rectangle Shape layer, it should have a new coordinate position of [0,0]. Now we should have something that looks like a slider, as that's basically what we are trying to achieve. Let's move the rectangle Shape layer to the bottom of the composition and bring in the pre-comp of the animation we made earlier into the composition.

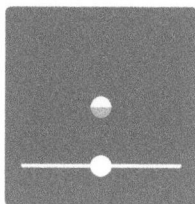

Now let's enable Time Remapping on the pre-composition we made earlier, which should add a Time Remapping property to the layer:

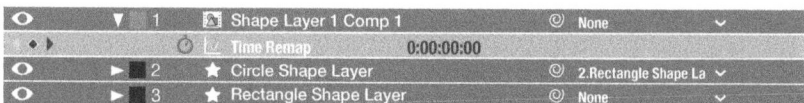

○		▼ 1	🖼 Shape Layer 1 Comp 1		◎ None ∨
◆ ►		○ Time Remap		0:00:00:00	
○		► ■ 2	★ Circle Shape Layer		◎ 2.Rectangle Shape La ∨
○		► ■ 3	★ Rectangle Shape Layer		◎ None ∨

Now I want the slider we just made to control the Circle animation, so when we slide it to the left, it goes to 0 sec of the animation and when we slide it to the right it goes to 1 sec of the animation. We know we can use the interpolation methods to convert one range of values to another, so let's write this expression in the Time Remap property of the pre-composition layer:

```
x = thisComp.layer('Circle Shape Layer').position[0];
linear(x,-400,400,0,1);
```

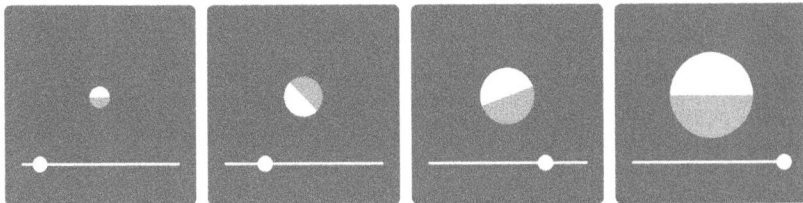

We created a variable, x, which calls the x position value of the circle Shape layer on the bar, then the **linear()** method converts the range of values of the position to a new range of values between 0 and 1. So, when we slide from left to right, the Circle animation will play between 0 and 1 second. Keep in mind that while the circle Shape layer has a position value of 0 on x in the middle of the bar, the **linear()** method that we used states that when it's at -400 on x it produces 0, and when it's at 400 on x it produces 1—the interpolation method will calculate the values in between.

You can move the circle Shape layer either with the mouse or manually when you change the parametric value of the position property, but we can see that it's not perfect because it can go beyond the bar:

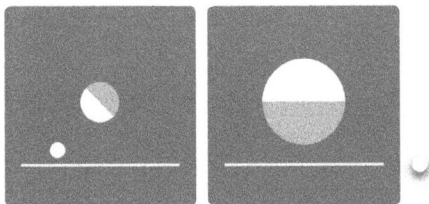

Let's make the circle stick to the bar, so that if someone else uses it, it will only be possible to move the circle in the slider to play the animation. We already know of a method that we can use to restrain values and prevent it from going over or under: **clamp()**. In the circle Shape layer, let's reveal the position property and write an expression:

```
x = clamp(value[0],-400,400);
y = 0;
[x,y];
```

The circle is now locked on the slider bar.

sourceTime()

As we can see, the circle on the bar behaves well as a slider - it controls the animation perfectly, whether we go forward, backward or pause it. I would like to show you one last thing about time in this chapter, to prove that what we are doing works well. I would like to display the time of the pre-composition animation in a Text layer.

We know that the animation goes from 0 sec to 1 sec, so when I move the slider it should display values between 0 and 1. Let's try this, create a new Text layer, and in the Source Text property write this expression:

```
thisComp.layer("Shape Layer 1 Comp 1").sourceTime();
```

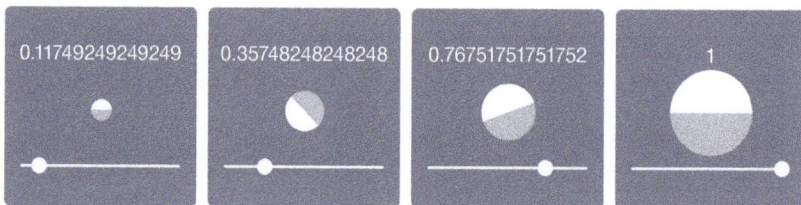

0.11749249249249   0.35748248248248   0.76751751751752   1

We can see it now displays the exact time of the animation which is controlled by the slider. I could have used the **time** value in the expression, but it would have produced the current time in the composition and not the current time of the animation. When you want to produce the actual current time of a layer and not that of the composition, you have to use the **sourceTime()** method instead, so when it's playing on the timeline and the layer is at 1 sec but the composition is at 2 sec, this will produce 1, and not 2.

In conclusion

To wrap up this chapter about the **time** value: we've seen how **time** can generate a continuous sequence of Number values, which defines one of the most interesting parts of Expression, a technology that will help make your animation smooth and effortless. It won't replace the keyframe work, but when you're in a rush or you want to improve your project, the combination of keyframes and expressions can offer you a whole new level of control and quality.

Space

The biggest part of animating in After Effects is moving layers within the composition, so linking the position values between layers, effects, etc. is something that happens quite often.

parent

The simplest way to link the position values of layers is to parent them:

When you parent one layer to another, it links the transform properties - the Anchor Point, Position, Scale and Rotation, all except for the Opacity property. The way parenting works is that it won't directly overwrite the parent values onto the child values, but will instead keep the child values while also following the changes applied to the transform properties of the parent values.

Note: if you want the values of the transform properties from the parent layer to overwrite the values of the transform properties from the child layer, you need to hold SHIFT while using the pick whip to parent the layers.

When you parent layers, you can use the term **parent** in the child layer, which behaves like a clone of the parent Object layer with all the same objects and values. For example, let's say we have LAYER B parented to LAYER A; go to the opacity property in LAYER B and enter this in the expression editor:

```
parent.opacity;
```

The opacity value of LAYER B will be linked to that of LAYER A, so all of the transform properties will ultimately be linked, which will help us to have fewer keyframes. You can still use all of the objects contained inside the parent layer, like effects, etc.

As usual, let's start by creating a new circle Shape layer in the middle of a composition, then add a new Solid layer. Let's apply a Radio Waves effect to this Solid Layer, which should look like this:

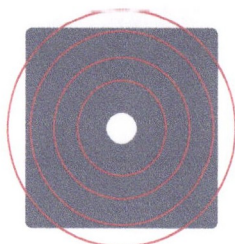

Let's say we want to always have the circle Shape layer at the center of the Radio Waves effect—to do this we can use the **parent** approach, as we saw in the previous example. Parent the circle Shape layer to the Solid layer, reveal the position property of the circle Shape layer and then write in the expression editor:

```
parent.effect("Radio Waves")("Producer Point");
```

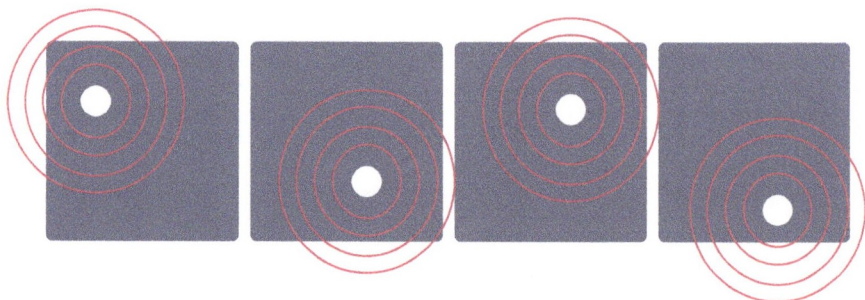

The position of the child layer will now have the same value as the Producer Point Object located in the parent layer, wherever we move the Producer Point. If the layers were not parented, we would have to write this in the expression editor:

```
thisComp.layer("Solid Layer").effect("Radio Waves")("Producer Point");
```

toComp()

Let's say the layers are not parented, so you'll have to use the last expression to link the position property of the circle Shape layer to the Producer Point. If we move the Solid layer with the effect to the right, the circle Shape layer will be offset from the Producer Point:

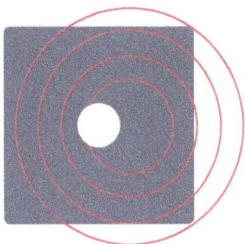

However, we want the circle Shape layer to always be at the center of the Radio Waves, no matter what transformations we apply to the Solid layer. Let's compare the different position values:

Circle Shape layer	[540,540]
Solid layer	[720,540]
Producer Point	[540,540]

It's pretty clear that the x axis of the Solid layer containing the Radio Waves effect is offset compared to the circle Shape layer. We might be tempted to add into the expression the difference between both layers, but we want to have the freedom to not have to rewrite the expression each time if we move the Solid layer again. Fortunately, we have a method in Expression that will make this kind of compensations for us, namely **toComp()**. Let's adapt the expression we have in the position property of the circle Shape layer:

```
x = thisComp.layer("Solid Layer").effect("Radio Waves")("Producer Point");
thisComp.layer("Solid Layer").toComp(x);
```

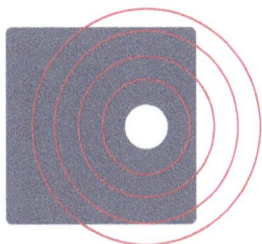

layer.toComp(point)

How does this work? The **toComp()** method works like a translator, taking the position value from inside a layer space and translating it to the equivalent position value in the composition space, just like if you wanted to project a location onto two different dimensions.

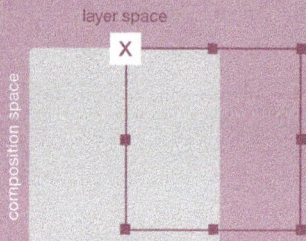

layer space

composition space

X

point x with a position value [0,0] in layer space will have a position value [540,0] in composition space

You first need to define which layer you want to translate to the composition space; then, using the **toComp()** method, you need to put as a argument the point or position value of the layer you want to translate onto the composition space. Just as in the example above, we call the position value [0,0] in the layer, and the method produces [540,0].

In our main example, the circle Shape layer is in the composition space, while the Producer Point is in the solid Layer space, so we have to translate the position value of the Producer Point in order to have them both in the same space. We first created a variable, x, which stores the position value of the Producer Point, then in the second statement we called the Solid layer which contains the effect and then applied the **toComp()** method. As an argument, we used the x variable that says which position value in the layer space we want to convert to composition space. In the end, the circle Shape layer is snapped to the Producer Point.

The great advantage of this method is that it works not only when we offset the position of the layer, but also if we change the anchor point, scale and rotation values:

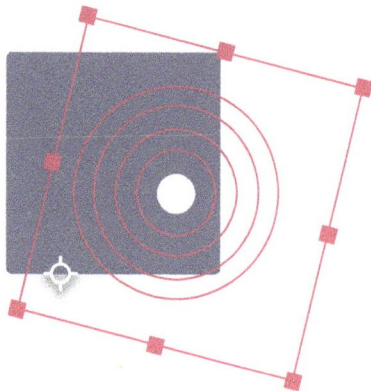

You can use the **toWorld()** method instead of **toComp()**, which will work the same way.

fromComp()

In the same way that we convert a position value from a layer space to a composition space, we can also convert a position value from a composition space to a layer space with the **fromComp()** method.
To demonstrate this, we will link the Producer Point value to the circle Shape layer, which will now be the Producer Point that follows the circle Shape layer (and not the contrary, as before). Let's remove the expression in the circle Shape layer position property and write an expression in the Producer Point property:

```
x = thisComp.layer("Shape Layer 1").transform.position;
thisLayer.fromComp(x);
```

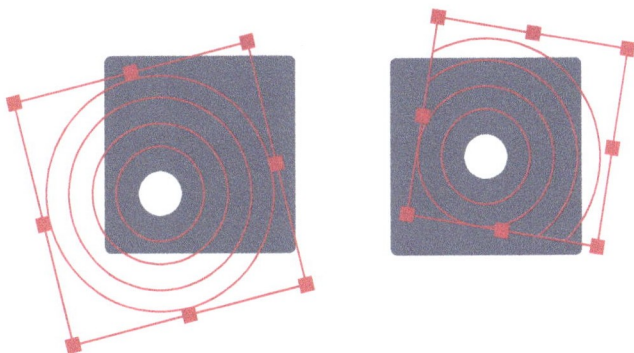

As you can now see, the Radio Wave Producer Point follows the circle Shape layer wherever the Solid layer is positioned. What did we do? We created a variable, x, which we assigned to the position value of the circle Shape layer, then called the object thisLayer, meaning we used the object where we wrote the expression—the Solid layer. Adding the **fromComp()** method to it, we used the variable x as an argument. The position value in the composition space is converted to the equivalent position value in the layer space.
We can see that the **fromComp()** and **toComp()** methods work in the same way—before using the method, you have to call the layer which defines the layer space to translate.

Because the expression lives in the same Object where we applied the method, we could have simplified it like this and removed **thisLayer**:

```
x = thisComp.layer("Shape Layer 1").transform.position;
fromComp(x);
```

You can also use the **fromWorld()** method instead of **fromComp()**, which will work in the same way.

fromCompToSurface()

In case the Solid layer is in 3D space, the **fromCompToSurface()** method will solve this:

```
x = thisComp.layer("Shape Layer 1").transform.position;
thisLayer.fromCompToSurface(x);
```

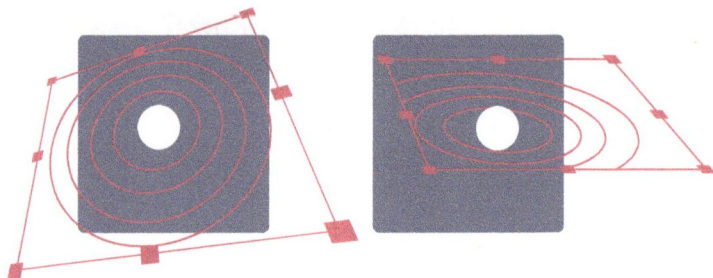

This works exactly same as the **fromComp()** method—the position value will be translated from composition space to the layer space in 3D.

These methods are really useful when you want to link effect properties to layers. You can link everything without the constraints of 2D, 3D or whether you move the layers, or if you want to link a value from a layer to the transform property of another layer, rather than a full parent-child relationship. Now that you have the full spectrum to link the position values of different objects and spaces together, you're not limited by space.

Layer space to Composition space
toComp() or **toWorld()**

Composition space to Layer Space
fromComp(), **fromWorld()** or **fromCompToSurface()**

Control

Expressions are not so easy to edit quickly, since you need to go into the expression editor to modify them. But what if you could control them through parametric values, just as you can do with effects? These tools work like a regular effect, but they're actually effects in the effect folder:

EFFECT ⟶ EXPRESSION CONTROLS ⟶ 3D Point Control
Angle Control
Checkbox Control
Color Control
Layer Control
Point Control
Slider Control

All of these controllers generate values. When you link them with expressions, think about **parametric expressions**.

Let's start by adding a circle Shape layer in a new composition:

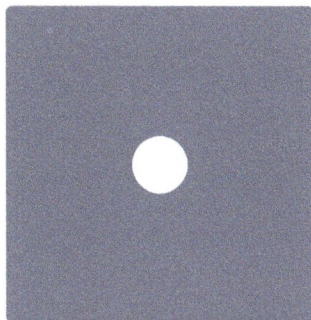

Point Control

Now I'd like to add a Point Control effect to this circle Shape layer. **A Point Control can produce an Array value of a point** the same as a layer with X and Y coordinates. The 3D Point Control produces an Array value with 3 values, so it's perfect for a property within a 3D environment (X,Y,Z).

Also, as a reminder, when you highlight an effect on the effect control panel and press enter, you can change its name:

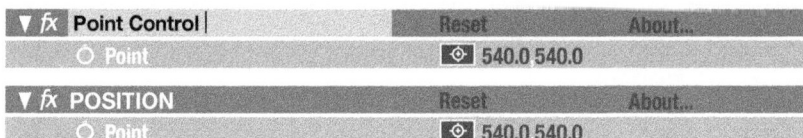

▼ *fx* Point Control	Reset	About...
○ Point	◈ 540.0 540.0	
▼ *fx* POSITION	Reset	About...
○ Point	◈ 540.0 540.0	

This is very useful to properly name the controllers, and keep your project clean—it'll be easier to edit, especially if someone else has to handle it.

Once we've renamed the Point Control as "POSITION", we want the position of the circle Shape layer to be linked to the Point Control effect. Let's reveal the position property of the circle Shape layer and write this expression:

```
effect("POSITION").param("Point");
```

We called the Object effect POSITION and we want to use the value of the Object "Point", so we'll use the Array value of this Object. Remember, by default an Object property will produce its **value**. So we can now control the position of the circle Shape layer directly from this Point Control effect.

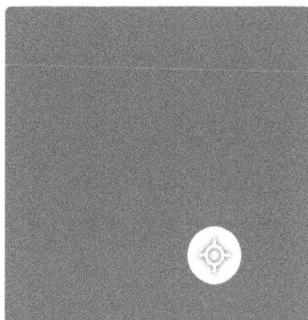

Color Control

Now I'd like to make the equivalent of a positive / negative test: if we move the circle Shape layer to the right side, it turns green; when it moves to the left side it turns red; and when it's in the center it goes back to white. Let's add three Color Control effects and two Slider Control effects to the circle Shape layer and rename them like this:

▼ fx POSITION	Reset	About...
Ò Point	🔾 540.0 540.0	
▼ fx CENTER COLOR	Reset	About...
Ò Color	▢ ▣	
▼ fx LEFT COLOR	Reset	About...
Ò Color	▥ ▣	
▼ fx RIGHT COLOR	Reset	About...
Ò Color	▨ ▣	
▼ fx GREEN AREA	Reset	About...
Ò Slider	700.00	
▼ fx RED AREA	Reset	About...
Ò Slider	300.00	

Next, let's reveal the Color property in the fill folder of the circle Shape layer and write this expression:

O		▼ ▣ 1	★ Shape Layer 1		
		▼ Contents		Add ❯	
O		▼ Ellipse 1	Ellipse 1	∨	
O		▼ Ellipse Path 1	▤ ➔		
O		▶ Fill 1	Normal	∨	
		Composite	Below Previous in Sa	∨	
		Fill Rule	Non-Zero Winding	∨	
		▶ Ò Color	▢ ▣		

```
leftArea = effect("RED AREA")("Slider");
rightArea = effect("GREEN AREA")("Slider");
centerColor = effect("CENTER COLOR")("Color");
colorLeft = effect("LEFT COLOR")("Color");
colorRight = effect("RIGHT COLOR")("Color");

if (position[0]< leftArea){
colorLeft;
}else if (position[0]>rightArea){
colorRight;
}else{
centerColor;
};
```

We can see that it's working pretty well—when we move the circle Shape layer to the left it turns red, and when we move it to the right it turns green, and when it's in the center it's white. So, what have we written?

Before explaining the expression, we'll add a Text layer so we can see what's going on, so let's write this expression in the Source Text property:

```
x = thisComp.layer("Shape Layer 1").content("Ellipse 1").content("Fill 1").color.value;
"r: " + x[0] + "\r" +"g: "+x[1] + "\r" + "b: " + x[2] + "\r" + "a: " +x[3] + "\r" ;
```

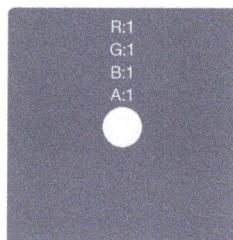

We created a variable, x, which we assigned to the color value of the circle Shape layer. This value is an Array, essentially an Array of 4 Number values between 0 and 1 that describe the Red, Green, Blue and Alpha channels. So for each number of this Array, we created a line to display these values—this is how colors work in expressions with an Array of 4 values.

Let's go back to the expression we wrote in the Color property: we created variables for each of the controllers: CENTER COLOR, LEFT COLOR, RIGHT COLOR, GREEN AREA and RED AREA.

```
leftArea = effect("RED AREA")("Slider");
rightArea = effect("GREEN AREA")("Slider");
centerColor = effect("CENTER COLOR")("Color");
colorLeft = effect("LEFT COLOR")("Color");
colorRight = effect("RIGHT COLOR")("Color");

if (position[0]< leftArea){
colorLeft;
}else if (position[0]>rightArea){
colorRight;
}else{
centerColor;
};
```

The leftArea and rightArea produce Number values from the Slider Control effects. To find out if the circle Shape layer is on the left or the right, we use the x position value of the circle Shape layer, so we can use the position value: position[0]. If we use the **if / else** conditional statement, we can compare **if** the x position value of the circle Shape layer is smaller than the leftArea value, the result will produce the colorLeft Array value, **else if** the x position value of the circle Shape layer is higher than the rightArea value, the result will produce the colorRight Array value. Finally, in the event that none of the conditions are true, the result of the expression will be the centerColor Array value.

You'll notice that with the conditional statement **if / else**, we can also add multiple conditions, in fact as many as you want:

```
If (condition 1)
{result 1}
else if (condition 2)
{result 2}
else if (condition 3)
{result 3}
else if (condition n)
{result n}
else
{result n+1}
```

Checkbox Control

▼ fx POSITION	Reset	About...
Ô Point	⊕ 540.0 540.0	
▼ fx CENTER COLOR	Reset	About...
Ô Color	▭	
▼ fx LEFT COLOR	Reset	About...
Ô Color	▭	
▼ fx RIGHT COLOR	Reset	About...
Ô Color	▭	
▼ fx GREEN AREA	Reset	About...
Ô Slider	700.00	
▼ fx RED AREA	Reset	About...
Ô Slider	300.00	
▼ fx ON / OFF	Reset	About...
Ô Checkbox	■	

Let's add another controller, a Checkbox Control effect, and rename it ON / OFF. The Checkbox Control is a pretty simple tool - when the Checkbox is checked it produces a Number value of 1, and when it's unchecked a Number value of 0.

I would like to make this Checkbox Control the ON / OFF button for the expression— if it's ON the color of the circle Shape layer will change, otherwise the expression won't be active. To do this we need to add a new conditional **if / else** statement into the expression that will contain the expression we previously wrote. If I wrote this by itself, it would look like this:

```
activeButton = effect("ON / OFF")("Checkbox");

if (activeButton == 1){
        result1;
        }else{
        result2;
        };
```

Now let's add this to the expression:

```
leftArea = effect("RED AREA")("Slider");
rightArea = effect("GREEN AREA")("Slider");
centerColor = effect("CENTER COLOR")("Color");

colorLeft = effect("LEFT COLOR")("Color");
colorRight = effect("RIGHT COLOR")("Color");

activeButton = effect("ON / OFF")("Checkbox");

if (activeButton == 1){
if (position[0]< leftArea){
colorLeft;
}else if (position[0]>rightArea){
colorRight;
}else{
centerColor;
};
}else{
centerColor;
};
```

Let's also add a line to the Text layer where it shows if it's ON or OFF. Edit the expression in the Source Text property like this:

```
x = thisComp.layer("Shape Layer 1").content("Ellipse 1").content("Fill 1").color.value;
y = thisComp.layer("Shape Layer 1").effect("ON / OFF")("Checkbox");

if (y == 1){
t = "ON"
}else{
t = "OFF"
};

"r: " + x[0] + "\r" +"g: "+x[1] + "\r" + "b: " + x[2] + "\r" + "a: " +x[3] + "\r" + t + "\r" ;
```

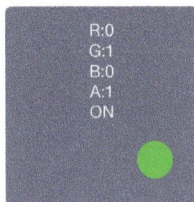

To the original expression, we added to the final value we produced the variable t, which is the result of the conditional statement **if / else** of the Checkbox Control. Now when we check or uncheck the Checkbox Control effect, we can see that the entire expression switches on or off.

Layer Control

Now when the circle Shape layer is on the right it turns green, and when it's on the left it turns red. Let's say we want to have some more options and have some circles gravitating around this circle Shape layer.
Let's create a new circle Shape layer, half the size of the main one.

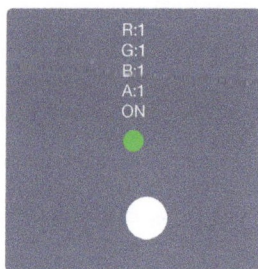

Next we'll add a Layer Control effect to the main circle Shape layer and rename it CHILD.

▼ fx POSITION	Reset	About...
Ō Point	⊕ 540.0 540.0	
▼ fx CENTER COLOR	Reset	About...
Ō Color		
▼ fx LEFT COLOR	Reset	About...
Ō Color		
▼ fx RIGHT COLOR	Reset	About...
Ō Color		
▼ fx GREEN AREA	Reset	About...
Ō Slider	700.00	
▼ fx RED AREA	Reset	About...
Ō Slider	300.00	
▼ fx ON / OFF	Reset	About...
Ō Checkbox	■	
▼ fx CHILD	Reset	About...
Layer	3. Shape Layer 1 ∨	Source ∨

The Layer Control effect allows us to select a layer in the composition, producing the Object layer selected. We will use this Layer Control like a parent layer, except it will do the reverse, so we'll make it select which Object is its child.

Let's reveal the position property of the new circle Shape layer and write this expression:

```
x = thisComp.layer("Shape Layer 1").effect("CHILD")("Layer");

if (x.name == thisLayer.name)
{thisComp.layer("Shape Layer 1").position;}
else
{value;}
```

We created a variable, x, which we assigned to the layer Object property of the Layer Control effect in the main circle Shape layer. A Layer Control produces an Object layer from the composition; remember, an Object can be defined by its name or its Index number. With the **if / else** conditional statement, when the Object has the same name as the layer where we write the expression, the layer will take the same position value of the main circle Shape layer; if it doesn't have the same name, it will take its initial position value.

R:1
G:1
B:1
A:1
ON

We can see that if we select the new circle Shape layer in the Layer Control, it links the layer to the main circle Shape layer, so this works. However, we also want it to be able to rotate around the main circle Shape layer. To do this, first we'll need to move the anchor point of the child circle Shape layer, therefore reveal the anchor point property of the child layer and write this expression:

```
x = thisComp.layer("Shape Layer 1").effect("CHILD")("Layer");
diameter = thisComp.layer("Shape Layer 1").content("Ellipse 1").content("Ellipse Path 1").size[0];

if (x.name == thisLayer.name)
{[diameter,0]}
else
{value;}
```

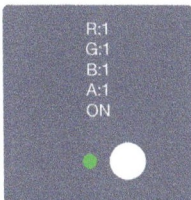

R:1
G:1
B:1
A:1
ON

This is just like the condition for the position, except we created a variable named diameter which we assigned to the width of the main circle Shape layer. An anchor point property has an Array of two values, which defines how near or far from the anchor point the layer is. Just as for the position, if the Layer Control selects the name of the layer, the anchor point will be offset by the diameter of the main circle; otherwise, it takes its initial value.

Angle Control

Lastly, we want to add an Angle Control effect on the main circle Shape layer which we will name CONTROL CHILD:

▼ fx POSITION	Reset	About...
Ö Point	⊕ 540.0 540.0	
▼ fx CENTER COLOR	Reset	About...
Ö Color	⬜ 🎞	
▼ fx LEFT COLOR	Reset	About...
Ö Color	🟧 🎞	
▼ fx RIGHT COLOR	Reset	About...
Ö Color	🟩 🎞	
▼ fx GREEN AREA	Reset	About...
Ö Slider	700.00	
▼ fx RED AREA	Reset	About...
Ö Slider	300.00	
▼ fx ON / OFF	Reset	About...
Ö Checkbox	■	
▼ fx CHILD	Reset	About...
Layer	3. Shape Layer 1 ⌄	Source ⌄
▼ fx CONTROL CHILD	Reset	About...
▶ Angle	0 x +0.0	

The **Angle Control effect** produces a Number value, which looks like its range only goes between 0 and 360 for the parametric value, but actually produces the number multiplied by the factor next to it. So, if you have 230*3, for example, it will produce 690. Having a parametric controller like this is really helpful if you want to work with degrees or to easily loop something.

Now I want the Angle Control effect to control the rotation of the child circle Shape layer, so let's reveal the rotation property of the layer and write this expression:

```
x = thisComp.layer("Shape Layer 1").effect("CHILD")("Layer");

if (x.name == thisLayer.name){
thisComp.layer("Shape Layer 1").effect("CONTROL CHILD")("Angle");
}else{
value;
}
```

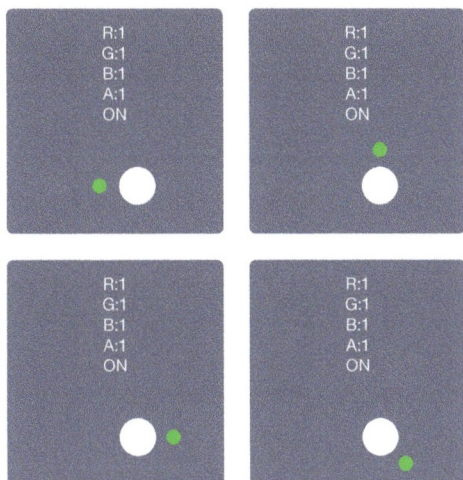

This is very similar to the expressions we wrote for the position and anchor point properties—we've said that if the Layer Control selects this layer, we want the value of the Angle Control effect to be the value produced; if not, it will take the rotation parametric value of the layer. As you'll see, we can now control the rotation of the child layer from the Angle Control effect of the main circle Shape layer.

Now we're going to see why we used the **thisLayer** object in these expressions.
If we duplicate the child layer, the copy will be a new option for us to use as a child of the main circle Shape layer, which is already set up. So, let's duplicate the child layer and make the copy red.

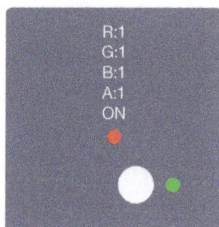

Then, using the Layer Control effect "CHILD", select the new Circle Layer and you'll now be able to switch them:

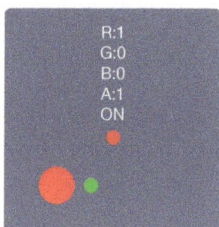

This gives us another option, and we don't even need to write expressions on it since we've used the term **thisLayer**; this is because when you use **thisLayer**, it calls the layer where the expression lives.

From the effects panel of the main circle Shape layer, you can control and play with the animation, just like in a template. The great thing about using these controllers is that they enable you to quickly modify your project without having to go into the properties of the layers and edit the expressions. Also, if someone needs to work on your project, it immediately points them towards where they can quickly edit the animation, whether they know how to use Expression or not.

Random

Earlier I introduced control—now it's time to present how to create chaos. Adding a touch of randomness to your animation is the little extra that makes your animation feel premium; it gives the illusion of life, and is also a great way of effortlessly generating values or motion.

First, let's create a circle Shape layer as usual:

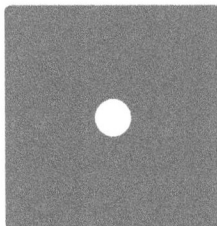

We're going to focus on the x position value to randomize the position of the circle Shape layer. Once again we want to display the x position value of the circle Shape layer on a Text layer, so let's create a new Text layer and in the Source Text property we'll write this expression:

```
Math.round(thisComp.layer("Shape Layer 1").position[0]);
```

What we did was to call the position value of the circle Shape layer, using the Array Index number [0] of the position value; remember, a position value is composed of two numbers and x has an Index number 0 in the Array. We then inserted this as an argument into the **Math.round()** method, because we want to produce a whole number for readability—we don't want a lot of decimals.

There are four methods we can use to randomize a value: **wiggle()**, **random()**, **gaussRandom()** and **noise()**.

wiggle()

First, let's talk about the superstar in the Expression world: **wiggle()**. This method is probably the first thing you'll hear about when discovering Expression for the first time— it's very easy to use, and you can drop it into almost any property. It also works with Number values or Array values, whether you have keyframes on the property or not, and it will seamlessly randomize the values without adding any extra terms.

Let's write this on the position property of the circle Shape layer:

```
wiggle(1,500);
```

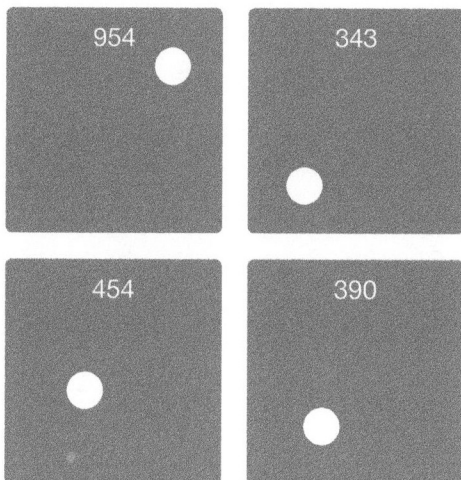

We can now see that the circle Shape layer is moving randomly in every direction. So, how does **wiggle()** work?

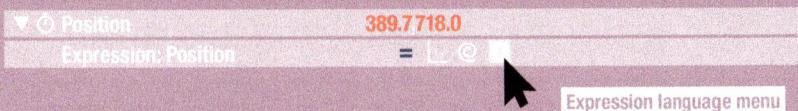

Position 389.7 718.0
Expression: Position =

Expression language menu

In the Expression language menu of After Effects, the wiggle method is presented like this:

wiggle(freq, amp, octaves = 1, amp_mult = .5, t = time)

When you choose a method from the Expression language menu, it shows you which arguments it needs. The arguments with an equals sign already have default values, which means if you don't specify them, they will be used this way by default.
For example:

wiggle(**freq, amp,** octaves = 1, amp_mult = .5, t = time)

We can see that we need to enter a minimum of two arguments for this method to work, freq and amp:

freq: This argument is the frequency, and like any regular frequency definition, it defines how many times per second the method will randomize the value. The higher the number, the more randomization you'll have per second.

amp: This argument is the amplitude. wiggle() calculates and randomizes the parametric value of the property within a positive and negative range, whether you have keyframes on the property or not. For example, if a rotation property has a parametric value of 100 and I enter an amplitude of 50, it will randomize the rotation value between 50 and 150.

octaves: This is an argument by default—if you don't enter anything, it will be 1. Like every randomized method, wiggle() is based on and calculated with noise, and just as with Fractal Noise or the other noise based effects, you can make the noise more defined. If you enter a higher number the noise will be more defined, and meaning you'll have more steps between the frequencies.

amp_mult: This is also a default argument, so if you don't enter anything it will be 0.5. It's the number of times the amplitude is multiplied for each octave, between 0 and 1. Like the octaves, the closer you are to 0 the less detail you'll have, and the closer you are to 1 the more detail you'll have.

t: This is another argument by default, and defines the time of the method you want to select. If you enter the time value, it will use the current time to randomize the value; if you enter 5, it will use the 5th second of the property to produce a randomized value, and this will continue throughout every frame.

The great thing about the **wiggle()** method is that it randomizes values that are next to each other throughout time, so it looks like it's interpolated. If it produces a value of -100 at second 1 then a value of 30 at second 3, between second 1 and second 3 it will also produce values that go from -100 to 30. You can put it on any property, as it will work, wherever there is a Number value or an Array value. For example, if you write a **wiggle()** method in a property, the same expression will work whether I write it on the rotation property, which needs to produce a Number value, or if I write it on the position value of a 3D layer that's an Array of 3 values. How does this work? Let me illustrate with the example we're using. For the circle Shape layer, with the **wiggle()** expression we have now, it's shaking in every direction (x and y), but as I mentioned I only want it to shake on the x axis. So, let's edit the expression on the position property with the **wiggle()**:

```
x = wiggle(1,100);
[x[0],value[1]];
```

623   546

As you can see, we created a variable, x, which stocks the **wiggle()** method; because a position property needs an Array value, the **wiggle()** will produce an Array. We then used the first value of the Array produced by the **wiggle()** with the Index number [0]. For the y position, we used the parametric value of the property, writing the term value[1], so the y position value should stay at 540.

Note that the **wiggle()** method is also based on the Index number of the layer, so if you move the layer to a different position in the hierarchy, the value produced will be changed. This is a very specific case, called the seed value, which can be controlled by the **seedRandom()** method. We know that for a layer the Index value starts from 1, but in this case the Index number will work like in an Array value and beginning the count in the hierarchy from 0, so by default it looks like this:

```
seedRandom(thisLayer.index - 1);
```

This is how it works, but the great thing about **seedRandom()** is that it offers you the possibility to choose from infinite possibilities—once you find the perfect one, you can simply keep the randomness, locking it with the Number value you entered as an argument in the **seedRandom()**. It's also worth noting that the seed value needs to be placed before the method. So, for our example we can write something like this:

```
seedRandom(42);
x = wiggle(1,1000);
[x[0],value[1]];
```

This will always produce the same range of values, whatever the rank of the layer in the hierarchy of the composition.

random()

The **seedRandom()** also works for other random methods. Let's see how it works with the next method: **random()**. In the position property of the circle Shape layer where we wrote the **wiggle()** expression, let's remove that expression and write this:

```
seedRandom(42);

x = random(1000);

[x,value[1]];
```

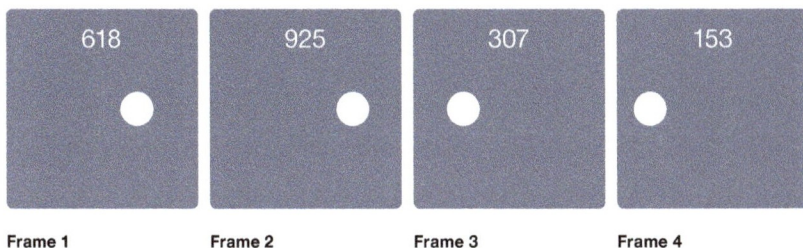

618	925	307	153
Frame 1	Frame 2	Frame 3	Frame 4

As we can see, at every frame it generates a new Number value between 0 and 1000. That's exactly how the **random()** method works.

random() // produces a random number between 0 and 1 at every frame

random(inputValue) /* produces a random number between 0 and inputValue at every frame */

random(inputValue 1,inputValue 2) /* produces a random number between inputValue 1 and inputValue 2 at every frame */

For the **random()** method, if the input value is a Number value it will produce a Number value; if it's an Array value it will produce an Array value.

seedRandom()

We've seen how the **random()** method produces a new value at every frame, which is where the **seedRandom()** comes in handy. In the expression language menu, the definition of the **seedRandom()** is:

seedRandom(offset, timeless=false)

As we can see, there is a second argument by default: timeless. This argument needs a Boolean value, either **true** or **false**. By default it's **false**, but you can also change it to **true**. What does this mean? **false** produces a new value at every frame, while **true** will produce a single value for the whole time.

```
seedRandom(42,true);

x = random(1000);

[x,value[1]];
```

618

The circle Shape layer will thus have a random value between 0 and 1000 and will keep this same value throughout the time. If you change the offset argument of the **seedRandom()** it will generate another random value, but as long as the second argument is **true** it will be one value throughout the entire time of the composition.

gaussRandom()

The **gaussRandom()** method is equivalent to the **random()** method, the only difference is that the random values that it produces will follow a Gaussian curve. This means that 90% of the results will be in the range of the input values, while 10% of results will be outside of this range of the input values.

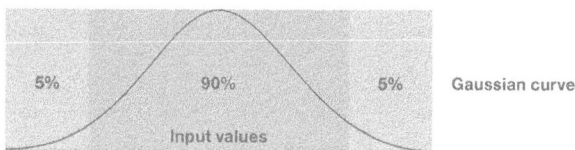

| 5% | 90% | 5% | Gaussian curve |

Input values

```
seedRandom(42,false);
x = gaussRandom(1080);
[x,value[1]];
```

For this expression, we will have 90% of the results between 0 and 1080, so inside the composition, and 10% of results out of this range, so outside of the composition.

noise()

The **noise()** method is somewhat similar to the **wiggle()** method, except it's not based on the seed value or the Index number, but rather on Perlin noise. Perlin noise is a type of noise that produces values between -1 and 1. The great thing about this method is that due to Perlin noise, the sequence of values produced will be numbers close to each other, so like the **wiggle()** method it will look like the frames playing are interpolated instead of jumping like in the **random()** method.

Since the **noise()** method is not based on the seed value or the Index number, it will always produce the same value for any number input as argument, for example:

```
noise(valOrArray)

noise(1); // Will always produce  -0.0153232799984
noise(2); // Will always produce  -0.0068915582945
noise(3); // Will always produce  0.01913710166916
noise(4); // Will always produce  -0.01711790583265
noise(5); // Will always produce  -0.0238015213381

etc.
```

If you want to create a sequence of values, we can use the **time** value as the argument to generate values through time, as in our example. Let's write this in the position property of the circle Shape layer:

```
x = noise(time)*1000;
[value[0]-x,value[1]];
```

Frame 1   Frame 2   Frame 3   Frame 4

noise(time) generates values between -1 and 1, so we created an x variable where we stock the result of the method multiplied by 1000, so that the movements will be more noticeable (as we're working with pixels). Finally, in the last statement where we write the result that will be produced, we created an Array where the variable x is subtracted from the parametric value of the x position, so that the circle Shape layer will move back and forth from the center, between -1000 and 1000 pixels. The other value in the Array will be locked on the parametric value of the y position.

posterizeTime()

The **noise()** method can create smooth animations because the values generated are very close to each other, like when we have keyframes interpolated. It's a quick and easy way to effortlessly generate animation. Now, let's say we want to randomize the randomization, and insert a **posterizeTime()** method as the first statement of the expression.

```
posterizeTime(5);

x = noise(time)*1000;
[value[0]-x,value[1]];
```

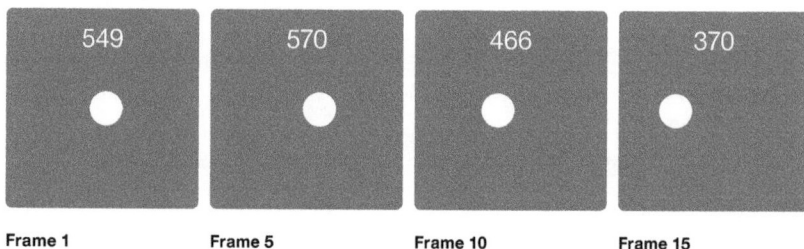

549	570	466	370
●	●	●	●

Frame 1   Frame 5   Frame 10   Frame 15

As we can see, it becomes like stop-motion—less smooth, only producing a new value every 5 frames, since 5 is the Number value we entered as argument in the **posterizeTime()** method. If you compare this to the values produced by the **noise()** method without the **posterizeTime()** method, it would be about the same value at the same time. **posterizeTime()** works as if it's changing the frame rate of the animation— if the project has 24 frames per second and you enter 12 as the argument of the **posterizeTime()**, it will change the value every 2 frames instead of every frame. If a lower Number value is entered as an argument, it will produce less values each second. Since the **posterizeTime()** method makes an operation between frames, the exactness of the values produced for the same frame, will be almost the same with or without the **posterizeTime()** method, but not identical.

posterizeTime() can also work if you have keyframes on the property and you want to have a stop-motion style: you just need to write the method on a statement before the final statement where the parametric value is produced:

```
posterizeTime(12);
value;
```

posterizeTime() can be a great way to bring some randomization into your animations or expressions. If you combined this term with the methods we saw previously—**wiggle()**, **random()**, **gaussRandom()** and **noise()**—you wouldn't need keyframes to work on properties. These methods are there to help you in your workflow, so you can quickly generate animation without having to use keyframes.

Condition

Condition is an essential part of creating behaviors in Expression. What is a behavior? Life usually gives us two options for every decision we have to make: accept or decline. Using conditions in Expression helps us define which result we want to produce, no matter what condition we face.

Boolean

In Expression, we know that accepting or declining is not a result, but we do have Boolean values, which produce **true** or **false** for a condition. Boolean values are how Expression compares statements and produces different values according to the conditions defined.

As usual, let's see how this works with a Text layer—create a new Text layer, and in the Source Text property let's type this in the expression editor:

```
10>9;
```

TRUE

```
9>10;
```

FALSE

As we can see, with Boolean values we can compare values. Here's another example, this time with a variable:

```
x = 10;
x>9;
```

TRUE

It's as simple as that—that's how conditions work. By comparing values, you'll be able to create conditions. A condition can be **true** or **false**, for example with the **time** value:

```
time > 4;
```

FALSE   TRUE

Before 4 sec.   After 4 sec.

Comparison operators

These operators are the mathematical tools we can use to compare two values. In our examples, we use the operator > which means 'greater than', but there are a lot more we can use:

> = Greater than or equal to

```
5 >= 5
```
TRUE

> Greater than

```
8 > 5
```
TRUE

<= Less than or equal to

```
5 <= 8
```
TRUE

< Less than

```
8 < 5
```
FALSE

!= Not equal

```
3 != 5
```
TRUE

!== Not equal in value and in type

```
"8" !== 5;
```
TRUE

== Equal

```
x = 8;
x == 5;
```
FALSE

```
x = "TEXT";
x == "TEXT";
```
TRUE

```
x = 10>9;
x == true;
```
TRUE

=== Equal in value and in type

```
"3" == 3
```
TRUE

```
"3" === 3
```
FALSE

Note: these comparison operators don't work with Array values.

Keywords

The keywords are the terms in Expression that allow us to verify a condition. We could summarize a condition like this:

Keyword (condition)
{result if the condition is true}

The result can be a value, a statement or an expression.

if

We've already come across the **if** keyword in this book, which is one of the most basic and frequently used keywords you'll see in Expression. It works as it sounds: **if** this is true, it produces this result. **if** usually works as a pair with another keyword **else**, but it can also work by itself.

In a new composition, let's add a new Red Solid layer, and in the opacity property of the layer let's write this expression:

```
t = 0;
if (time>1)
{t = 100;};
t;
```

Before 1 sec.   **After 1 sec.**

Using **if** in the expression means a new value will be produced if the current time is greater than 1 second, but if it's under 1 second, the condition will be **false**—it won't have anything to produce and will produce an error if we haven't defined a value before the condition. So, when we want to use an **if** conditional statement, we first need to define what value is to be produced before the condition is verified. In our case, we created a variable, t, that we assigned the value 0; when the condition is **false** it will produce the same value as before testing the condition, and only if it's **true** will it produce the new result for the variable t.

if / else

if can be very useful when you only want something to work if the condition is **true**, as the value produced before the **if** statement will remain unchanged if this condition is **false**. We've also seen the **if / else** conditional statement, which works in a similar way. For this, we don't need to define a value by default, we basically just define the two results:

```
if (condition 1)
{result 1}
else
{result 2};
```

We don't need to define the second condition because the first condition already defines the second—it's either **true** or **false**. For example, let's write this in the opacity property of the Red Solid layer:

```
if (time>1){
100;
}else{
0;
};
```

Before 1 sec.   **After 1 sec.**

As you can see, we just wrote the **if / else** in a different way. This is how programmers write it in JavaScript—as you'll remember, lines and spaces don't matter, only the semi-colon close the statement. You can space out your expression however you want, but I wanted to show you it written this way because it's the most common way for other Expression users to write the **if / else** conditional statement. **if / else** is one of the most frequently used conditional statements, so it's worth getting used to it.

Conditional ternary operator: ?

When you only have one condition, such as **if / else**, there's a faster way of writing it—the conditional ternary operator. This is not so commonly used, but it can fit on one line, and when your expression is getting a bit long regarding statements, it can be a great way of simplifying it. Here's how it works:

```
(condition)? result 1: result 2;
```

This means that if the condition is true, it will produce result 1; if it's false, it will produce result 2. Let's see how this works in our example:

```
(time>1)? 100 : 0;
```

Different aspect, same result. So, now you're fully prepared to take the decision between two options.

Logical operators

We can be more specific within the condition by adding more comparisons to the condition, thanks to logical operators.

&& means **and**—we need two comparisons to be true in order to verify the condition, for example:

```
(time >1 && rotation == 0)? 100 : 0;
```

If the time is greater than 1 second *and* the rotation of the layer is 0, the condition will be true, producing 100. Otherwise, if neither of these or only one of them fits the condition it will be false, producing 0.

|| means **or**—if either of the comparisons is true, this will produce a true answer:

```
(time >1 || rotation == 0)? 100 : 0;
```

So, if the current time is greater than 1 second *or* the rotation of the layer is equal to 0, it will produce 100; if neither of these are true, it will produce 0.

! means **not**, and needs to be placed before the condition:

```
!(time > 1)? 100 : 0;
```

When the time is *not* greater than 1 second it will produce 100, while if time is greater than 1 second it will produce 0.

else if

Now, we want to add more conditions, we can use the **else if** keywords to add more conditions to the statement, which would look something like this:

```
if (condition 1)
{result 1}
else if (condition 2)
{result 2}
else if (condition 3)
{result 3}
else if (condition 4)
{result 4}
...
else if (condition n)
{result n}
else
{default result};
```

Let's try this with the Red Solid layer example—write this expression in the opacity property:

```
if (time < 1){
0;
}else if (time >= 1 && time < 2){
20;
}else if (time >= 2 && time < 3){
40;
}else if (time >= 3 && time < 4){
60;
}else if (time >= 4 && time < 5){
80;
}else{
100;
};
```

| 0 sec. | 1 sec. | 2 sec. | 3 sec. | 4 sec. | 5 sec. |

With the **else if** keywords, you're not limited by the number of conditions—you can add just one, or as many as you want.

switch

Another way we could achieve this is to use the **switch** keyword:

```
switch (Math.floor(time)) {
default:
100;
break;
case 0:
0;
break;
case 1:
20;
break;
case 2:
40;
break;
case 3:
60;
break;
case 4:
80;
break;
};
```

This looks pretty self-explanatory and similar to the **if / else** conditional statement, but there are some differences that need to be defined.

First, we rounded the **time** value with the **Math.floor()** method. This method rounds a decimal number to the smaller of the two closest whole numbers, so for example everything between 1 sec and 2 sec will be rounded down to 1. We need this to count the time beginning from 0, so between 0 sec and 1 sec this method will produce 0, then 1, 2, 3, etc. We use this value as an input in the **switch** keyword; this is how, the **switch** keyword works, instead of having a condition we have an input:

```
switch (input) {
default:
result default;
break;
case 0:
result 0;
break;
case 1:
result 1;
break;
...
case n:
result n;
break;
};
```

case

The input entered in the **switch** keyword needs to be a Number value. So if the input equals 0, it will produce the result 0; if it's 1 it will produce the result 1, etc. How do we define this? With the **case** keyword:

```
switch (X) {
case X:
result X;
break;
```

The value in the input will be the one that determines which **case** the **switch** has to use, so if the input value is 1, it needs to use **case** 1. Like the **else if** keywords, you can use as many instances of **case** as you want.

If the **switch** statement doesn't find a **case** to use, the **switch** statement will use the **default** keyword, producing a **default** result; usually, the **default** needs to be placed first, before any instance of **case**:

```
switch (X) {
default:
result default;
break;
```

In order to use a **case** or a **default**, it works as a block, like this:

```
case X or default:
result X;
break;
```

The **case** doesn't need to be placed in order—if you put **case** 4 before **case** 1, it will still work fine within the **switch** statement. Also; if two or more instances of **case** produce the same value, you can group them together like this:

```
switch (Math.floor(time)) {
default:
100;
break;
case 3:
case 4:
40;
break;
case 1:
case 2:
80;
break; }
```

break

The **break** keyword tells the expression to stop looking for a result when it finds a **case** that is true. Essentially, how it works is that the **switch** tests every block until it finds a **case** that's true, after which it will produce the corresponding result, then break out of the **switch** statement thanks to the **break** keyword. As you'll see, we can also use it in other conditional statements. You need to use it within the **switch** statement, otherwise it will keep testing the next **case** forever. So, every time you add a **case**, you also need to add a **break** statement afterwards.

Assignment operators

As you'll remember, the = sign assigns a value to a variable and the == sign verifies if two values are equal. An = is an assignment operator, while a == is a comparison operator, just as with comparison operators, there are different types of assignment operator. These assignment operators will reassign a value to a variable.

Let's create a variable t:

```
t = 100;
```

+=

Addition assignment operator

```
t = 100;
t += 1; // It will produce 101
```

t+=1	is the same as	t = t + 1

-=

Subtraction assignment operator

```
t = 100;
t -= 1; // It will produce 99
```

t-=1	is the same as	t = t - 1

*=

Multiplication assignment operator

```
t = 100;
t *= 1; // It will produce 100
```

t*=1	is the same as	t = t * 1

/=

Division assignment operator

```
t = 100;
t /= 1; // It will produce 100
```

t/=1	is the same as	t = t / 1

%=

Remainder assignment operator

```
t = 100;
t %= 1; // It will produce 0
```

t%=1	is the same as	t = t % 1

We assign a value to a variable, then with the assignment operator we can reassign a value to the variable by using a math operation. These operators will be useful because they allow us to manipulate the variables with the conditions.

Increment and decrement operators

These two operators work in the same way as assignment operators; in fact, they *are* assignment operators, they're just a common shortcut to write it faster.

++

Increment operator

```
t = 100;
t++;
t; // It will produce 101
```

t++	is the same as	t+=1	is the same as	t = t +1

The increment operator is a shortcut to reassign +1 to a variable.

▬ ▬

Decrement operator

```
t = 100;
t--;
t; // It will produce 99
```

t--	is the same as	t-=1	is the same as	t = t -1

The decrement operator is a shortcut to reassign -1 to a variable.

These operators are useful because they allow us to simplify our writing in the expressions.

while

Let's reuse our Red Solid layer, and write this expression in the opacity property:

```
x = 0;
t = 0;
while (x <= time)
{ t += 10;
x++
};
t;
```

As we can see, the opacity of the Red Solid layer increases by 10% every second.

To clarify: when you need to manipulate variables, you have to create them; the **while** keyword that we created needs at least two variables to work, so we created x and t, to which we assigned the Number value 0. t will be used to produce a result, and x will be used to determine the condition. **while** works like a loop; to illustrate, here's an example of a loop:

```
x = 0;
t = 0;

while (x <= 6){
t += 10;
x++;
};

t;
```

one loop

```
      ┌─ x = 0:  t = 0    t = t + 10   t = 10
  x++ ├─ x = 1:  t = 10   t = t + 10   t = 20
  x++ ├─ x = 2:  t = 20   t = t + 10   t = 30
  x++ ├─ x = 3:  t = 30   t = t + 10   t = 40
  x++ ├─ x = 4:  t = 40   t = t + 10   t = 50
  x++ ├─ x = 5:  t = 50   t = t + 10   t = 60
  x++ └─ x = 6:  t = 60   t = t + 10   t = 70
```

x = 7 the condition is false.

So, the final result is the last one
t = 70

As we can see above, the loop performs the statement t+=10 for every step while x is less than or equal to 6, until it reaches 6 for each step of x++. In the end, we produce the variable t.

Two general rules you'll need to remember when using a loop like **while**:

1

Expression calculates the result to produce for the property at every frame. Expression doesn't have a memory, so the result of the previous frame isn't stored anywhere.

/* you can create a variable and reassign a new value to this variable, but ultimately the value of this variable will be the last reassignment.*/

2

t = 1;
t = 23;
t = 42*10;
t++;
t = 0;

t; //will produce the last assignment which is 0

The **while** statement works like a loop, going through every condition until the condition is false. So in our example, let's say the current **time** is 6 seconds:

```
x = 0;
t = 0;
while (x <= time)
{ t += 10;
x++
};
t;
```

Condition x = 0, t will produce 10
Condition x = 1, t will produce 20 (or previous result +10)
Condition x = 2, t will produce 30 (or previous result +10)
Condition x = 3, t will produce 40 (or previous result +10)
Condition x = 4, t will produce 50 (or previous result +10)
Condition x = 5, t will produce 60 (or previous result +10)
Condition x = 6, t will produce 70 (or previous result +10)
After 6 seconds, the condition is false.

The second statement, x++, is the step statement that defines how it checks and performs the condition at every step—because we put an increment operator ++, it will perform the condition +1 again and again until the condition is false. If we change the step statement to +2, it would look like this:

```
x = 0;
t = 0;
while (x <= time)
{ t += 10;
x += 2;
};
t;
```

Condition x = 0, t will produce 10
Condition x = 2, t will produce 20 (or previous result +10)
Condition x = 4, t will produce 30 (or previous result +10)
Condition x = 6, t will produce 40 (or previous result +10)
After 6 seconds, the condition is false.

The great thing is that the **time** value generates a sequence of Number values at a regular frequency, so at every frame, **while** will do another loop and calculate a new result. The combination of **time** and **while** can simulate having a cache memory in Expression, which mimics saving the previous results from past frames.

As we can see, **while** performs all of the conditions until it reaches a false condition, performing the statement or expression over and over again until the condition is false, after which it will produce the last result of the loop. We could summarize the **while** statement like this:

```
x = 0;
y = value;

while (x <= value){
statement or expression producing y;
step x;
};

y;
```

We can also make the step statement the first statement—just make sure to always add a step statement when you use the **while** keyword, otherwise it won't work.

```
while (condition){
step;
statement or expression;
};
```

do / while

The **do / while** statement works in exactly the same way as the **while** keyword by itself, the difference is that you have to define the expression that needs to be performed before testing the condition. So, for our example it would look like this:

```
x = 0;
t = 0;
do {
t += 10;
x++
}
while (x <= time);
t;
```

The same thing will happen to the Red Solid layer—the opacity increases by 10% every second. So, if we were to make a basic template for the **do / while** statement it would look like this:

```
do {
step;
statement or expression;
}
while (condition);
```

for

The **for** statement also works as a loop, but it may be faster to use because you write the condition and the step statement directly inside the parentheses—only the statement or expression to be performed is inside the curly brackets. Our example, where the opacity of the Red Solid layer increases by 10% every second, would look like this:

```
x = 0;
t = 0;

for (x; x<= time; x++) {
t += 10;
};
```

As we can see, to use the **for** keyword we need to define three statements inside the parentheses: first, which variable we will be comparing (this first one is optional—if you don't write anything, it will work anyway); second, the actual condition; and third, the step statement. These all need to be separated by semicolons, so it looks like three distinct statements:

```
for (statement 1; statement 2; statement 3) {
statement or expression;
};
```

also can be written like this:

```
for (; statement 2; statement 3) {
statement or expression;
};
```

continue

As we've seen earlier, **while, while / do** and **for** keywords work like a loop, testing all of the conditions until the condition is **false**. We also saw how with the **switch** keyword, we need to use the **break** keyword, which tells the expression to break out of the **switch** after the result is performed. We can also use the **break** keyword to exit a loop—let's write this in the opacity property of the Red Solid layer:

```
x = 0;
t = 0;

for (x; x <= time; x++) {
if (x == 1) {break;}
t += 10;
};
t;
```

As you can see, inside the expression to perform, we've added this condition:

> if (x == 1) {break;}

This means that after the keyword starts its loop and reaches the condition x = 1, it will then exit the loop. In this way, the loop will never go past the point where the condition x = 0, so the opacity will remain at 10%. The **continue** keyword also allows us to skip one condition in the loop:

```
x = 0;
t = 0;

for (x; x <= time; x++) {
if (x == 1) {continue;}
t += 10;
};
t;
```

This time we used this condition:

> if (x == 1) {continue;}

This means that every time the keyword loops through the expression, when the condition x = 1 is true, it will skip it and not perform a result for this condition. In our example, it won't increase the opacity by 10% at second 1, instead it will increase it by 10% at second 2 and above.

So, **break** tells the expression to exit the loop, and **continue** tells it to skip a condition.

for / in

The **for / in** statement is a little different than all the other past keywords: So far, we've compared the values and produced **true** or **false** for a condition using comparison operators. However, for this one we need to use the **in** operator, which will also produce **true** or **false** if a value term (property / attribute) exists in an Object, which is how it loops within an Object. Let's recreate our example with this statement—to make our Red Solid layer increase its opacity by 10% every second, let's write this in the opacity property:

```
var array1 = [time*10,10];
var t = 0;
var x;

for (x in array1){
Math.floor(t += array1[x]*0.1)*10;
};
```

We created an Array value with two values (remember, an Array value behaves like an Object). array1[0] is **time***10, and the second value is 10. As for the other keywords, we then created a variable, t, which we used to produce a result; variable x is used to make the **for / in** statement work.

When we write **for** (x **in** an Array or an Object){**we need to have the Array or Object in the result, followed by the square bracket with the variable x in it, instead of an Index number**}. This x will loop inside all of the values of the Array value or the Object, thus performing the result as many times as there are values. In our case, we have an Array value with two values, so it will run the statement twice. Let's see what happens if the **time** is 1 second on the timeline:

t = Math.floor(t += array1[x]*0.1)*10;

one loop
| t = Math.floor(t += array1[0]*0.1)*10; | t = Math.floor(t += (time*10)*0.1)*10; | t = 10 |
| t = Math.floor(t += array1[1]*0.1)*10; | t = Math.floor(t += 10*0.1)*10; | t = 20 |

The final result at 1 sec. will be t = 20

Since **time** is a value that produces a Number value in decimal, we need to use the **Math.floor()** method to round the decimal number down to the closest, smallest whole number. We then want to have an increment every second, not in between—the math operation, multiplied by 0.1 then by 10, helps to fix this.

As we can see, the variable x will be the element that loops inside the length of the Array or Object:

```
var x;
var y = value;

for (x in Array or Object){
y += statement with Array[x] or Object[x];
};
```

Express Yourself

Text layer

So far in this book, we've used the Text layer as a way of displaying the result of the expressions we write and to check if things work as we wanted. But when it comes to manipulating actual text in animations, there are an infinite number of possibilities available with the range selector and animation properties you'll find next to the Object group: Text.

Sometimes, however, there will be a situation where, among the infinite possibilities, you can't find the solution you're looking for. Fortunately, a **String value**, like a **Number value** or an **Array value**, can be manipulated through methods or operations, so allow me to show you with a simple example how adding a bit of Expression to the text can easily save you from needing a ton of keyframes.

Typing

Let's say we want to animate a text to look like you're typing something on your computer, so the letters appear one by one with a vertical bar at the end of the last letter typed. You could do this by using the opacity and character value in the text animator, but to achieve this would take a lot of keyframes and adjusting, and every time you needed to change the text, you'd have to redo it.

Let's make an expression that won't need any keyframes, which will work with whatever text you enter:

sourceText

Let's create a new Text layer and type "Express yourself":

Express yourself

Now let's reveal the Source Text property and open the expression editor; by default, this is shown:

```
text.sourceText
```

sourceText is the Object property that contains the **String value** we manually entered using the type tool; for example, if you write rotation in the **rotation** property, it produces the parametric value. So, **sourceText** is how we call the manually typed text. Let's create a variable which stocks this:

```
txt = text.sourceText;
```

Character value

We can operate on a **String value** like an **Array value**. A **String value** is a group of characters where the count of the first character starts from 0, just like the **Array Index number**, and the space counts as a character. So, for our example:

E	x	p	r	e	s	s		y	o	u	r	s	e	l	f
0	1	2	3	4	5	6	7	8	9	10	11	12	13	14	15

slice()

Now I'd like to have the letters appear one at a time. To achieve this, we need a method that can cut the String value, and the **slice()** method can do just that. This method needs two arguments:

slice(Start,End)

Start is a Number value that indicates the character number where the Text begins, while End is a Number value that indicates the character number where the Text ends. For example:

```
txt = text.sourceText;
txt.slice(0,1);
```

E

I used the **slice()** method beginning at 0, before the E, and ending at position 1, after the E, so we only show the E.

length

```
txt = text.sourceText;
txt. slice(0,txt.length);
```

Express yourself

length is a value of the sourceText Object that produces the total number of characters in the String value; "Express yourself" has 15 characters, so **txt.length** should produce the Number value 15. We start before the E with the Number value 0, and end at the Number value 15, which is the exact number of characters in the sentence; so, it now shows all of the characters.

If you guessed that by animating the second argument in the **slice()** method we would be able to show the characters one at a time, you're right. We could use a **Slider Control effect** to generate a Number value to animate the second argument, but we want to go without keyframes, so let's take advantage of the **time** value to generate a Number value from 0.

```
txt = text.sourceText;
txt.slice(0,time);
```

Ex	Exp	Expre	Express

This works—it adds a letter every second, but this is way too slow, so it doesn't seem like someone is typing. We at least need to be able to decide when the animation ends—we could multiply the time by a Number value to make it faster, but to truly control the time, we want to be able to decide when this animation ends. I want the animation to happen for 1 second, beginning at 0 seconds. This can be done using a **linear()** interpolation method, which will convert the range of the **time** value into the range of the value we need for the second argument in the **slice()** method:

```
txt = text.sourceText;
speedTxt = linear(time,0,1,0,txt.length);
txt.slice(0,speedTxt);
```

Ex	Express	Express yo	Express yourself

The **linear()** interpolation method means that when the time is at 0 seconds it produces a Number value of 0, and when the time is at 1 second it produces the exact number of characters in the text, thanks to the **length** value. By doing this, the animation lasts exactly 1 second. If in the future we want the animation to start later, end sooner (or even later), we just need to edit these arguments in the **linear()** interpolation method—this way, it's easy to edit.

To make things clearer, let's create a variable and name our final Text anim:

```
txt = text.sourceText;
speedTxt = linear(time,0,1,0,txt.length);
anim = txt.slice(0,speedTxt);
```

As we mentioned before, I want it to look like someone typing on their computer, so it needs a vertical bar at the end, after the most recent character in the animation:

```
txt = text.sourceText;
speedTxt = linear(time,0,1,0,txt.length);
typeMark = "|";
anim = txt.slice(0,speedTxt);
anim+typeMark;
```

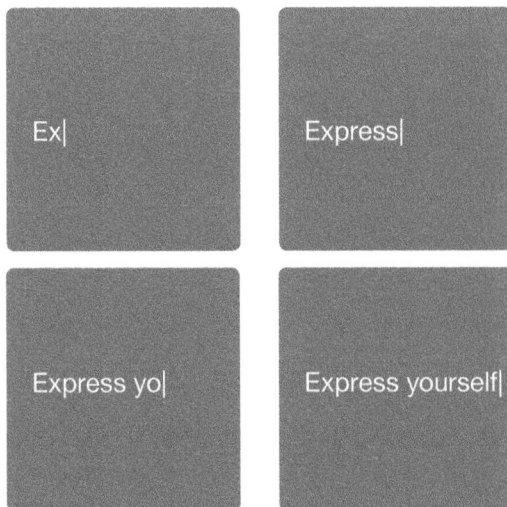

Ex|

Express|

Express yo|

Express yourself|

I created a variable, which I named typeMark, where I assigned a String value "|". Remember, you can add String values by using the + mathematic operator, just as you do with Number values. In the last statement, I want it to produce the anim variable + the typeMark variable, which means that when it produces the String value "Express yourself", for example, it will add the String value "|" at the end of the last character. By doing this we will always have the String value "|" after the most recent character throughout the duration of the Text animation.

We almost have it, and without too much effort, now we just need to add one last finishing touch. I want the vertical bar sign to only appear when it's typing, so how can we achieve this? We already know the final **length** of the text, so we can use a simple **if / else** conditional statement to indicate that if the current **length** of the Text is less than the final **length** of the Text, it will add the vertical bar after the Text, otherwise it will simply produce the Text by itself:

```
txt = text.sourceText;
speedTxt = linear(time,0,1,0,txt.length);
typeMark = "|";
anim = txt.slice(0,speedTxt);

if (speedTxt < txt.length){
anim + typeMark;
}else{
anim;
};
```

Expre|

Express yourself

Perfect! As you can see, to make the condition we just have to reuse the variable speedText, which actually produces the current **length** of the text and compares it with the **length** of the Source Text. When the speedTxt is less than the **length** of the Source Text it produces the addition of the anim variable + typeMark variable; when the speedTxt is not less than the **length** of the Source Text, it just produces the anim variable, i.e. the final text without the vertical bar.

Every situation is different, but knowing you can play with the **String value** and achieve this sort of thing by using expressions gives you another advantage that should set you at ease when you start a project, confident you can achieve the result you really want. Knowing the possibilities of using expressions on top of regular effects or preset animations can really expand your repertoire of what you can create.

toLowerCase() and toUpperCase()

Now when the Text is animating I want it to be lower case, then when it's finished I want it to be upper case. On the String values, you can apply the **toLowerCase()** and **toUpperCase()** methods—apply these to the results in the condition **if / else**:

```
txt = text.sourceText;
speedTxt = linear(time,0,1,0,txt.length);
typeMark = "|";
anim = txt.slice(0,speedTxt);

if (speedTxt < txt.length){
f = anim + typeMark;
f.toLowerCase();
}else{
anim.toUpperCase();
};
```

expre|

EXPRESS
YOURSELF

replace()

Let's go even further and say that when it's finished animating, you want it to reveal the text "Amaze yourself". There is a method that can find a word within a String value and replace it with another word:

replace(a,b)

The **replace()** method needs two arguments—a is the String value you want to find, and b is the String value you want to replace it with. In our example:

```
txt = text.sourceText;
speedTxt = linear(time,0,1,0,txt.length);
typeMark = "|";
anim = txt.slice(0,speedTxt);

if (speedTxt < txt.length){
f = anim + typeMark;
f.toLowerCase();
}else{
anim.replace("Express","Amaze").toUpperCase();
};
```

ex|

express|

express yo|

AMAZE YOURSELF

Global replacement

Note that this **replace()** method is case sensitive, which means it will try to find the same word with the same upper and lower case letters, so I had to write the word to find exactly how I originally typed it: Express, with a capital E. You can avoid this by using global replacement, for which you need to put the first argument between **/ .. /gi**, without the quotation marks:

replace(/a/gi,b)

So, in our example:

```
txt = text.sourceText;
speedTxt = linear(time,0,1,0,txt.length);
typeMark = "|";
anim = txt.slice(0,speedTxt);

if (speedTxt < txt.length){
f = anim + typeMark;
f.toLowerCase();
}else{
anim.replace(/express/ig,"Amaze").toUpperCase();
};
```

Now let's duplicate the sentence three times:

ex|

express yourself
expre|

express yourself
express yourself
express yo|

AMAZE YOURSELF
AMAZE YOURSELF
AMAZE YOURSELF

As you can see, the animation still works and replaces the three Express words in the same text block. The **replace()** method without global replacement only replaces the first word found in the block text. However, if you use global replacement, **/ ... /g** or **/ ... /gi** it will replace all the String values it finds in the text block with the new String value.

/ ... /g case sensitive global replacement
/ ... /gi non case sensitive global replacement

The String value, which is the Text, can be a truly rich source of creativity—if you keep working at it, you'll amaze yourself with the infinite combinations you can create by mixing the text animator tools with Expression. More importantly, this can save you a tremendous amount of time in some projects.

Loop

Saving time

We've seen how with the **time** value, we can easily generate quick animations, which is a timesaver when we have a ton of animation to do. Another way of saving time is by using loops, which are not only super useful but also allow you to create seamless animations.

By definition, loops repeat a sequence—we already know valuable methods to perform this in Expression:

Math.cos() and Math.sin()

First, as we saw in the Time chapter, we can make a loop using the **Math.cos()** or **Math.sin()** methods, because as we've seen, Cosine and Sine generate a repeating sequence of values between -1 and 1 over time. For example, if I apply this expression in the position property of a circle Shape layer:

```
[thisComp.width/2,thisComp.height/2+Math.cos(time*10)*100];
```

On the x axis, we wrote that we want the circle Shape layer to be positioned at half the width of the composition, and for the y axis to be positioned at half the height of the composition; we then add the Cosine method to the y position. In the **Math.cos()** method we use **time** as an argument, which we then multiply by 10 so that the frequency is 10 times faster. We know this method generates a sequence of values between -1 and 1, so we multiply it by 100 to produce values between -100 and 100, so that the circle Shape layer will go back and forth between -100 pixels and 100 pixels from the center of the composition over time. This produces a perfect, seamless loop going back and forth from one point to another.

% operator

We have another mathematical way of creating a loop: the modulo operator %. This operator is a computing operations that produces the remainder of a division between two positive whole numbers:

A%B produces the remainder of the division of A divided by B.

For example:

0/5	will have a remainder of 0	7/5	will have a remainder of 2
1/5	will have a remainder of 1	8/5	will have a remainder of 3
2/5	will have a remainder of 2	9/5	will have a remainder of 4
3/5	will have a remainder of 3	10/5	will have a remainder of 0
4/5	will have a remainder of 4	11/5	will have a remainder of 1
5/5	will have a remainder of 0	12/5	will have a remainder of 2
6/5	will have a remainder of 1	etc.	

As you can see, this loops the divisor; in our example 5 is the divisor, so every time the dividend is a multiple of 5, it will return to 0. This can be very useful in our expressions. Let's add a square Shape layer to a new composition, and a Text layer where we will display the rotation value of the rectangle Shape layer, then write this expression in the Source Text property:

```
thisComp.layer('Shape Layer 1').rotation;
```

Now, in the rotation property of the rectangle Shape layer, let's add this expression:

```
(time*100)%180;
```

As we can see, this causes the rotation of the rectangle to loop when it reaches 180, returning it to 0. If you combine **time** with a modulo operation, you can create a loop that will repeat itself over time. Luckily, we have a much easier way to produce a loop, thanks to the loop methods.

Loop methods

First, let's create a circle Shape layer on a 5 second composition, and make a quick animation so that the circle Shape layer moves from left to right. Let's add a first keyframe on the position property [250,540] and a second keyframe 20 frames later at [800,540].

Now reveal the expression editor in the position property of the circle Shape layer and from the expression language menu, find the **loopOut()** method:

▼ ○ Position 250.0 540.0
Expression: Position = 〰 ◎ ▸

Expression language menu

Property >> loopOut(type = "cycle", numKeyframes = 0)

This is a great menu that can help you find the terms to build the expressions. Within this menu, under the Property folder, let's select the **loopOut()** method: as you can see, the menu helper writes the method with the arguments fully detailed in the expression editor. If you now play the animation, you'll see that after the last keyframe, it loops out of the animation and returns to the first keyframe.

When we remove the arguments inside the method: loopOut();

We can see that it doesn't change anything—the same loop occurs. As I mentioned earlier, if the arguments written with an equal sign in a method are left unchanged or if nothing is inserted, these will be the arguments used by default. So essentially, the following expressions will work in the same way:

loopOut(type = "cycle", numKeyframes = 0);

loopOut(type = "cycle");

loopOut("cycle", 0);

loopOut("cycle");

loopOut();

Note that if you want to modify the second argument, you also need to enter the first argument, even if you want to use the default one.

loopOut()

The **loopOut()** method allows you to loop the sequence of keyframes in a property, after the last keyframe.

In this method, the first argument you can enter is a **String value**. There are 4 types of String values you can use in this method: **"cycle"**, **"pingpong"**, **"continue"** and **"offset"**.

Let's say the first keyframe is A and the second keyframe is B:

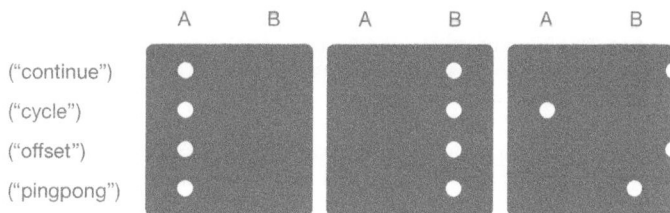

loopOut("continue")
After it reaches keyframe B, the animation will continue the movement with the same speed and direction as it had in the keyframe B.

loopOut("offset")
After it reaches keyframe B, it begins the loop from B and will play A to B starting from B; the following loops will then be played starting from the previous offsets.

loopOut("cycle")
After it reaches keyframe B, it will restart from A.

loopOut("pingpong")
After it reaches keyframe B, it will play in reverse, from B to A.

This is easy to understand when the property only has two keyframes; however, sometimes the property has more than two keyframes, and this is where the second argument in the method, **numKeyframes**, is useful. The Number value you enter is the number of keyframes you want to loop after the last keyframe in the property. If it's 0, it will loop all the keyframes in the property; if it's 1, it will only loop one keyframe before the last keyframe; if it's 2, it will loop the 2 keyframes prior to the last keyframe, and so on. For **loopOut()** remember that it loops from the last keyframe.

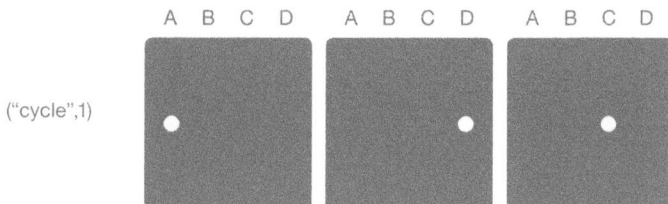

If you want to call the number of keyframes in a property, you can use **numKeys**. In the example above, if we write **thisProperty.numKeys** in the position property, it should produce the Number value 4, because there are 4 keyframes.

You're ready

There are other methods available for creating loops on properties with keyframes—**loopOutDuration()** works in the same way, except the second argument to enter in the method is not the number of keyframes to loop after the last keyframe, but rather the duration in seconds from the last keyframe. The **loopIn()** and **loopInDuration()** methods have the same applications, but start from the first keyframe of the property and loop the animation before the first keyframe, and then stop the loop after the last keyframe of the property.

All these loop approaches provide us with fast, smooth ways of creating animations with just a few expressions. They are small things, but if you can apply them in your After Effects projects each day, you'll find they help you to gain rhythm. More importantly, you'll have more time to think creatively about your project.

During the course of this book, we've studied how to read and write Expression, using some built-in terms. Expression is an ever-expanding universe, with every new update for After Effects adding new built-in terms that can be used with Expression. We could, for example, have mentioned the new Path Objects to enter Expression in a path and control the points of a path or a mask with Expression, among many other features. However, now that you have the tools to understand this on your own and can see how Expression works, you can adapt yourself to any situation, develop your own expressions and understand other people's work.

To close this chapter, I'd like to return to the **loopOut()** method we saw earlier. As you'll remember, methods are functions, as we saw in the Insight chapter. I'd like to show you how it could have looked if we had to write our own **loopOut()** function. This function, as you'll see in the next few pages, would work in exactly the same way as the **loopOut()** method. Try it—drop it onto any property, and you'll see it behaves in the same way. Obviously, **loopOut()** is much quicker to use; I only wanted to show you this because, thanks to everything you've learned in this book, you're now able to build this expression, to read it, and to see that what may first appear a giant mass of code is in fact made from just a few terms, where only the logic of transferring values matters. My mission in this book was to lighten things up a little—now you can face it without fear, and meditate on how it can help your After Effects workflow.

What if we had to build the **loopOut(type = "cycle", numKeyframes = 0)** method as a function, working with the exact same arguments? I've made all of the terms we've encountered throughout this book darker—you don't need to know anything else to understand this, as you'll see:

```
function newLoopOut(a,b){
x = thisProperty.numKeys;

if ((a=="cycle" && b==null) || (a==null && b==null) || (a=="cycle" && b==0)){

if (thisProperty.key(x).time<time){
loopDuration = thisProperty.key(x).time - thisProperty.key(1).time;

r = linear(time,thisProperty.key(x).time,thisComp.duration,0,thisComp.duration-
thisProperty.key(x).time);

newTime = linear(r%loopDuration,0,loopDuration,thisProperty.key(1).
time,thisProperty.key(x).time);

return thisProperty.valueAtTime(newTime);

}else{
return thisProperty.value;
};
}else if (a=="cycle" && b>0){
if (thisProperty.key(x).time<time){
loopDuration = thisProperty.key(x).time - thisProperty.key(x-b).time;

r = linear(time,thisProperty.key(x).time,thisComp.duration,0,thisComp.duration-
thisProperty.key(x).time);

newTime = linear(r%loopDuration,0,loopDuration,thisProperty.key(x-b).
time,thisProperty.key(x).time);

return thisProperty.valueAtTime(newTime);

}else{
return thisProperty.value;
};

}else if ((a=="pingpong" && b==null) || (a=="pingpong" && b==0)){

if (thisProperty.key(x).time<time){
loopDuration = thisProperty.key(x).time - thisProperty.key(1).time;

r = linear(time,thisProperty.key(x).time,thisComp.duration,0,thisComp.duration-
thisProperty.key(x).time);

r1 = r%loopDuration;

t = linear(r1,0,loopDuration,1,-1);

r2 = r%(loopDuration*2);

t2 = linear(r2,0,loopDuration*2,1,-1);
```

```
if (t2<=0){
remapTime = -1*t
}else{
remapTime= 1*t
};

newTime2 = linear(remapTime,-1,1,thisProperty.key(1).time,thisProperty.key(x).
time);

return thisProperty.valueAtTime(newTime2);

}else{
return thisProperty.value;
};
}else if (a=="pingpong" && b>0){
if (thisProperty.key(x).time<time){
loopDuration = thisProperty.key(x).time - thisProperty.key(x-b).time;

r = linear(time,thisProperty.key(x).time,thisComp.duration,0,thisComp.duration-
thisProperty.key(x).time);

r1 = r%loopDuration;

t = linear(r1,0,loopDuration,1,-1);

r2 = r%(loopDuration*2);

t2 = linear(r2,0,loopDuration*2,1,-1);

if (t2<=0){
remapTime = -1*t
}else{
remapTime= 1*t
};

newTime2 = linear(remapTime,-1,1,thisProperty.key(x-b).time,thisProperty.
key(x).time);

return thisProperty.valueAtTime(newTime2);

}else{
return thisProperty.value;
};
}else if (a=="continue"){

if (thisProperty.key(x).time<time){

newTime = linear(time,thisProperty.key(x).time,thisComp.duration,0,thisComp.
duration-thisProperty.key(x).time);
t = thisProperty.key(x).time;
y = thisProperty.velocityAtTime(t-framesToTime(1));
```

```
if (t<time){
if (typeof y == "object"){
if (y.length == 3){
return [value[0]+y[0]*newTime,value[1]+y[1]*newTime,value[2]+y[2]*newTime];
}else{
return [value[0]+y[0]*newTime,value[1]+y[1]*newTime];
};
}else{
return [value+y*newTime];
};
}else{
return value;
};
}else{
return thisProperty.value;
};
}else if ((a=="offset" && b==null) || (a=="offset" && b==0)){

if (thisProperty.key(x).time<time){

loopDuration = thisProperty.key(x).time - thisProperty.key(1).time;

r = linear(time,thisProperty.key(x).time,thisComp.duration,0,thisComp.duration-
thisProperty.key(x).time);

newTime = linear(r%loopDuration,0,loopDuration,thisProperty.key(1).
time,thisProperty.key(x).time);

step = linear(Math.floor(r/loopDuration),0,thisComp.duration,0,loopDuration*
thisComp.duration);

offset = linear(step,0,loopDuration*thisComp.duration,1,thisComp.duration+1);

path = thisProperty.valueAtTime(newTime);

offset2 = thisProperty.key(x).value-thisProperty.key(1).value;

return offset*offset2+path;

}else{
return thisProperty.value;
};
}else if (a=="offset" && b>0){
if (thisProperty.key(x).time<time){

loopDuration = thisProperty.key(x).time - thisProperty.key(x-b).time;

r = linear(time,thisProperty.key(x).time,thisComp.duration,0,thisComp.duration-
thisProperty.key(x).time);
```

```
newTime = linear(r%loopDuration,0,loopDuration,thisProperty.key(x-b).
time,thisProperty.key(x).time);

step = linear(Math.floor(r/loopDuration),0,thisComp.duration,0,loopDuration*
thisComp.duration);

offset = linear(step,0,loopDuration*thisComp.duration,1,thisComp.duration+1);

path = thisProperty.valueAtTime(newTime);

offset2 = thisProperty.key(x).value-thisProperty.key(x-b).value;

return offset*offset2+path;

}else{
return thisProperty.value;
};
};

}

newLoopOut("cycle");
```

Bonus

New Expressions Engine: JavaScript

During the production of this book, Adobe After Effects released an update of its software with a new **Expressions Engine: JavaScript**. It's one of the biggest updates made to the expressions system since the old legacy ExtendScript engine. This update increases the power to everything we have learned so far, not only is the engine faster than ever but we now have access to more methods, keywords, operators and a lot of other tools from todays modern JavaScript language. In this chapter we will discover new features that not only help maintain simplicity and readability in our expressions but also allow us to discuss something very important that we haven't yet mentioned: Optimization.

Multi-line String value

Throughout this book, we have used the String value in order to understand how expressions work. With this new engine, the String value has also received new features that allow us to manipulate them easier. For example, as you remember when we wanted to write a text on multiple lines, we had to use the String value **"\r"** which produces a text action to go to the next line. Within this new version, it becomes much easier, all we have to do is use the backtick:`. Simply write your text between backticks and you don't even need to use the quotation marks, everything inside will be interpreted as a String value.

```
"Text"+"\r"+ "Text"+"\r"+ "Text";
```
is the same as
```
`Text
Text
Text`
```

Note that you can also use the backtick approach as a substitute to the quotation marks for the String value:

```
"text" === `text`;
```
```
thisComp.layer("Layer 1").position;
```

is the same as

```
thisComp.layer(`Layer 1`).position;
```

New methods for String values

One of my favorite things to do, is to explore the Expression world by using a well-known function that can reveal the values and methods available in an Object.

For example, let's create a new Text layer and write this expression in the Source Text property:

```
x = [];

function getKeys(object){
var keys = "";
for (var x in object){
keys += x + "\r";
};
return keys;
};

getKeys(thisProperty);
```

className
toString
valueOf
valueAtTime
charAt
charCodeAt
concat
endsWith
fromCharCode
includes
indexOf
lastIndexOf
localeCompare
match
repeat
replace
search
slice
split
startWith
substr
substring
toLocaleLowerCase
toLocaleUpperCase
toLowerCase
toUpperCase
trim
values
propertyGroup
key
nearestKey

As we can see this function uses a **for / in** statement to loop in an Object and therefore can produce every element inside the Source Text Object. Right away we can see that there are new terms available: the methods **concat()**, **endsWith()**, **includes()**, **repeat()**, **startsWith()** and **trim()** are now present in this new engine. These new terms are well-known JavaScript methods that can be used to manipulate a String value.

"My text".concat(" is complete","!"); /* will produce My text is complete! Add one or multiple String values */
"My text".startsWith("My"); /* will produce true. Check if the String value starts like the argument entered */
"My text".endsWith("t"); /* will produce true. Check if the String value ends like the argument entered */
"My text".includes("text"); /* will produce true. Check if the argument entered exists in the String value */
"My text".repeat(2); /* will produce My textMy text. Repeat the String value as many times as the Number value entered as argument */
"   My text   ".trim(); /* will produce My text. Trim the white space at the beginning and at the end of the String value */

New methods for Array values

Like the String values, the Array values also have some notably new useful methods.

Regular methods:

[1,2,3,4,5].fill(1,1); /* will produce 1,1,1,1,1. This method fills the Array with a value entered as the first argument and the second argument is the Array Index number where it starts to fill the Array Value */

[1,2,3,4,5].copyWithin(1,0,1); /* will produce 1,1,3,4,5. This method copies a segment within the Array and keeps the same length. The first argument is the Index number where it starts to overwrite the segment in the Array. The second argument is the Index number of where the segment copy starts and the third argument is where it ends */

[1,2,3].includes(4); /* will produce false because the value 4 doesn't exist in the Array value */

[1,2,3].indexOf(3); /* will produce 2 which is the Index number of value 3 in the Array, if the value doesn't exist in the Array it will produce -1 */

Methods that produce Array iterator Objects:

var x = [1, 2, 3];
test = x.entries(); /* will produce an Array Iterator Object for each Index number with their corresponding values in the Array value */
test.next().value; /* will produce 0,1 which is the value of the first Array iterator Object */
test.next().value; /* will produce 1,2 which is the value of the second Array iterator Object */
test.next().value; /* will produce 2,3 which is the value of the third Array iterator Object */

r = [1, 2, 3].keys() /* will produce an Array iterator Object for only each Index number in the Array value */
r.next().value; /* will produce 0 which is the value of the first Array iterator Object */
r.next().value; /* will produce 1 which is the value of the second Array iterator Object */
r.next().value; /* will produce 2 which is the value of the third Array iterator Object */

Methods using callback functions:

find(), **findIndex()**, **forEach()**, **filter()**, **find()**, **reduce()**, **some()** and **every()**. A Callback function is a function that can be used as as an argument in another function. They're a great substitute for loops, since they are more readable. For example:

```
r = [1,2,3];

s = r.map(function(a){return a * 2});

s;
```

2,4,6

Instead of

```
r = [1,2,3];

for (let x = 0; x<r.length ; x++){
r[x] *= 2;
};

r;
```

2,4,6

map() method produces a new Array value from the callback function that individually operates on the values of the Array value.

New Methods For Math Object

```
Math.random(); /* will produce random Number values between 0 and 1 at every frame */
Math.hypot(2,3) /* will produce the hypotenuse of a right triangle given as arguments the measurement of the opposite and adjacent sides */
```

var, let and const

Now it's time to think about optimization. So far, we really haven't had the chance to think about this aspect of our expressions, mostly because the examples used in this book are pretty light and optimizing them would only speedup the calculations by milliseconds which wouldn't be too noticeable. However when you have a big project with a lot of expressions or want to make a very advanced expression, having good habits can really boost the speed of the calculations. Making your expression hyper responsive rather than slow. Similar to when you need to find the right balance within the assets and effects of a project in order to have a reasonable render time.

As you remember Expression doesn't have memory, well *it* doesn't but there are some tricks that make the engine work in the background as best possible. As we have seen with the **var** keyword, a variable can be global or local depending of where you declare it. For example if you declare a variable with a **var** keyword in a function it will become a local variable which means it will only exist in the function. If you declare it outside of the function with the same **var** keyword, this variable will be global. With the new engine, we can now use the **let** and **const** keywords to create a variable. A big advantage of using **let** and **const** is that they're already providing precious information in terms of readability:

```
let x = 10; // we create the variable x
x = 11; // we can reassign 11 to the variable x
```

```
const x = 10; /* we create the variable x but can't reassign a value to it, it's in read-
only. You can use it as a regular variable but never reassign it */
```

Therefore when you see a **let** or a **const** variable in an expression you receive extra information regarding the use of the variable and whether or not it can be reassigned. Meanwhile a **var** variable doesn't provide any information of this kind. A second great aspect of **let** and **const** is that they declare the variables block-scoped, which means they will only exist in the expression where it's declared, similar to a local variable declared in a function. Let me show you an example:

Create a Text layer in a composition and write this in the expression editor of the Source Text property:

```
var Variable1 = 10;
let Variable2 = 10;
const Variable3 = 10;
```

Then create a new composition, and in this new composition, create a Text layer and write this in the Source Text property:

```
x = [];

let getKeys = function(object){
    var keys = "";
    for (x in object){
        keys += x + "\r";
    };
    return keys;
};

getKeys($.global);
```

```
thisLayer
thisProperty
__internal_expression_state
__internal_err_code
__internal_err_msg
Variable1
x
```

As you can see we have re-used the function to get the values and methods of an Object. The $ Object stocks diverse information about the Expression system of your project, and inside there is the global Object, we can see the variables that it retains in the background. As we can see, the **Variable1** from the previous composition created with **var** is there, but without the other variables. We can also see that the variable **x** from the expression above is there too. We have proved that the variables created with **let** and **const** don't travel further than where they live in their expression. Ok, let's confirm that point and rewrite this actual expression.

```
let getKeys = function(object){
    let x = [];
    var keys = "";
    for (x in object){
        keys += x + "\r";
    };
    return keys;
};

getKeys($.global);
```

```
thisLayer
thisProperty
__internal_expression_state
__internal_err_code
__internal_err_msg
Variable1
x
```

We now declared the variable **x** with the **let** keyword and also moved it inside the function but nothing has changed.

Let's try to remove these variables from the engine with the **delete** keyword:

```
let getKeys = function(object){
let x = [];
var keys = "";
for (x in object){
keys += x + "\r";
};
return keys;
};

getKeys($.global);

delete x;
```

true

```
let getKeys = function(object){
let x = [];
var keys = "";
for (x in object){
keys += x + "\r";
};
return keys;
};

getKeys($.global);

delete Variable1;
```

false

```
let getKeys = function(object){
let x = [];
var keys = "";
for (x in object){
keys += x + "\r";
};
return keys;
};

getKeys($.global);
```

```
thisLayer
thisProperty
_internal_expression_state
_internal_err_code
_internal_err_msg
Variable1
```

By declaring the **x** variable with the **let** keyword, we were able to remove it, but not the **Variable1** declared with **var**. The point of seeing this, is that even though these variables are not usable, they still exist in the background. For small expressions this doesn't have a great impact but when you have a lot of complex expressions this can be a fundamental part in slowing down the calculations, therefore using now **let** and **const** to declare a variable is not only useful for readability but also for optimization when you want to have better performances.

Object constructor

In this book, we've seen how to create our own Object, and how to use the values (or properties / attributes) of this Object in the expression. We have also seen that Objects, like layers, can be called with the **layer()** method in **thisComp** Object. Since we already know how to create a function in order to make operations on values, let's learn how to use a function to create single or multiple Objects:

```
function Layer(anchorPoint, position, scale, rotation, opacity) {
    this.anchorPoint = anchorPoint;
    this.position = position;
    this.scale = scale;
    this.rotation = rotation;
    this.opacity = opacity;
};

myLayer = new Layer([0,0],[540,540],[100,100],0,100);
myLayer.position; // will produce 540,540

myLayer2 = new Layer([100,222],[1040,700],[100,100],0,50);
myLayer2.opacity; // will produce 50
```

Using the **this** keyword allows us to create a customizable Object. As you remember, **this** takes the form of the Object container, therefore the Object we create from the function will have its values inherited from the arguments entered in the function. Then by using the **new** keyword we can create single or multiple Objects from the same function. This approach can be very useful if we need to create multiple Objects in the same After Effects property. With this new Expressions Engine, you can also create an Object using the class constructor approach:

```
let Layer = class {
    constructor(anchorPoint, position, scale, rotation, opacity) {
        this.anchorPoint = anchorPoint;
        this.position = position;
        this.scale = scale;
        this.rotation = rotation;
        this.opacity = opacity;
    } };
myLayer = new Layer([0,0],[540,540],[100,100],0,100);
myLayer.position; // will produce 540,540
```

Another enhancement for the Objects that comes with this new engine is the simplicity of adding a value (or property / attribute) to an Object without necessarily using the pair nameValue: value. You can now directly add a value to an Object this way:

Old engine

New engine

```
x = 10;
newObject = {x:x};
newObject.x; // will produce 10
```

```
x = 10;
newObject = {x};
newObject.x; // will produce 10
```

Arrow functions

The way of writing functions has also been simplified with the implementation of arrow functions. Take a look at this example:

```
let myFunction = (a) => a + 2;

myFunction(2); // will produce 4
```

is the
same as

```
let myFunction = function(a){
return a+2 ;}
myFunction(2); // will produce 4
```

Looks much more readable!

FunctionName = (arguments) => expression to produce;

Default arguments

Another great new feature for building functions is the presence of default arguments. With the old engine we had to use an **if** statement inside the function in case the argument was not inserted when calling the function:

Old engine:

```
function TEST(a,b){
if (b==null){
b = 10;};
return a + b;}

TEST(10); // will produce 20
```

We now have two new ways of declaring the default value for an argument:

New engine:

```
function TEST(a,b){
var b = b || 10;
return a + b;}

TEST(10); // will produce 20
```

or

```
function TEST(a,b=10){

return a + b;}

TEST(10); // will produce 20
```

As you can see, we can declare the default argument inside the function using the || logical operator, and we can also declare it directly inside the parentheses where we declare the arguments.

Rest and spread operators

The rest and spread operators ••• are another new way of simplifying your expressions and avoiding extra steps. The rest operator comes especially handy with functions. In order to understand this, we first need to see something we haven't encountered before: the **argument** term. This term produces an Array value that can be used inside the functions to store the arguments of the function:

```
function TEST(a,b){
return arguments[0];
}

TEST(1,2); // will produce 1
```

```
function TEST(a,b){
return arguments[1];
}

TEST(1,2); // will produce 2
```

The rest operator is somewhat similar, with the exception that you do not have to define how many arguments your function can receive:

```
function TEST(...args){
return args[0];
}

TEST(1,2); // will produce 1
```

```
function TEST(...args){
return args[1];
}

TEST(1,2); // will produce 2
```

The spread operator will do the reverse of the rest operator and transform the Array value into singles values:

```
function createArray(...val){
return val;
};

Array1 = createArray(10,30,5,170,32,90);

Math.max(...Array1); // will produce 170
```

We've created a function in which multiple values can be entered as arguments. We now want to know the highest Number values between these numbers. For this we can use the **Math.max()** method however it only accepts Number values, we can solve this by using the spread operator to convert our Array value to Number values.

Destructuring assignment

The destructuring assignment is an easy and quick way to create variables from an already existing Object or Array.

First create a new Text layer and type TEXT, then write the following in the expression editor of the Source Text property:

```
value; // will produce TEXT
speed; // will produce an undefined value
velocity; // will produce an undefined value
name; // will produce the name of the Object layer: TEXT
```

Now look at what happens when we write the destructuring assignment as a first statement:

```
let {value,speed,velocity,name} = position;

value; // will produce 540,540
speed; // will produce the current speed position of the layer
velocity; // will produce the current velocity position of the layer
name; // will produce the name of the Object property: Position
```

You can see that the values are now inherited from the Position Object, and not from the Source Text Object where the expression lives.

{value terms} = Object container

The same approach works for Array values:

```
let x = [200,100,50];

let [a,b,c] = x;
a; // will produce 200
b; // will produce 100
c; // will produce 50
```

[variables] = Array Value

for / of

In this new engine, the **for / of** statement is a loop we can add to our list of tools that can loop through an Object. It's very similar to the **for / in** statement, however the **for / of** statement is more purposeful for looping through the values of a String value or an Array value:

```
function ADDITION(...args) {
let total = 0;
for (let arg of args) total += arg;
return total;
}

ADDITION(1,2,3,4); // will produce 10
```

Test

Now let's put to use the new tools we've learnt in this chapter to see how the new Expressions Engine will significantly improve the performance of the expressions. We are going to do an advanced expression that not only would have been harder to execute but also would have taken longer to calculate in the old engine.

We are also going to take advantage of this example to use the new Path expression terms so we can control the points of a mask or a shape. For this example, we will work on a mask but this can work on any kind of path such as a shape layer.

First, it's good to understand how a path works in expression. In a new composition, add a Solid layer. In this Solid Layer, just draw or add any kind of mask so that the Masks folder appears in the hierarchy.

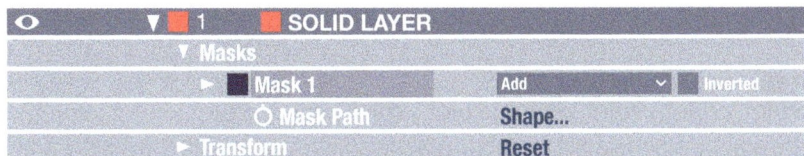

⊙	▼ ▦ 1	▦ SOLID LAYER			
	▼ Masks				
	► ▦ Mask 1		Add	⌄	Inverted
	○ Mask Path		Shape...		
	► Transform		Reset		

Now that we can see the Mask Path property, let's open its expression editor and select the **createPath()** method in the Expression language menu:

> Path Property > createPath(points = [[0,0], [100,0], [100,100], [0,100]], inTangents = [], outTangents = [], is_closed = true)

This **creatPath()** method from the Mask Path Object is more simple than it looks. The first thing to remember is an Array value can contain other Array values and it's exactly the type of arguments that we need to fill in with this method. Let's look at the details to see which arguments are needed:

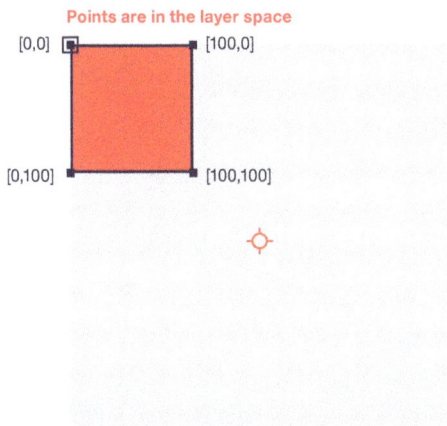

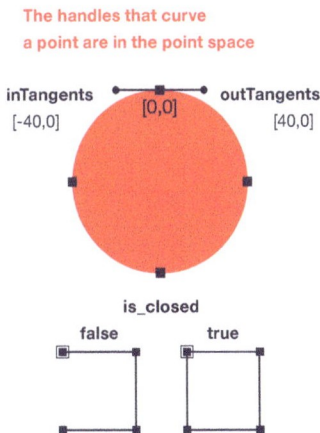

Points are in the layer space

[0,0] ▪━━━━━━▪ [100,0]

[0,100] ▪━━━━━━▪ [100,100]

◇

The handles that curve a point are in the point space

inTangents ●━━▪━━● outTangents
[-40,0]   [0,0]   [40,0]

is_closed

false   true

At this point we have a square generated by the **creatPath()** method, but let's say we want to generate a circle, actually let's generate a couple of them. We know that only one path per Mask Path property can be generated but if the Mask with the expression is duplicated, it would also duplicate the circle mask. By adding a random method it can automatically place the duplicated circle in a new position. There are a lot of arguments needed for this **createPath()** method and we want to be able to control the position and radius of the circle, as we saw earlier an Object constructor can create a new Object where we can enter arguments so let's try using an Object constructor for this:

```
/* OBJECT CONSTRUCTOR */

function circle(x,y,diameter) {
    this.x = x;
    this.y = y;
    this.diameter = diameter;

{
circle.prototype.create = function() {
let positionCircle = [this.x,this.y];
let diameter = this.diameter;
const tang = 3.8;
let a = [positionCircle[0],positionCircle[1]-diameter/2];
let b = [diameter/2+a[0],diameter/2+a[1]];
let c = [a[0],diameter+a[1]];
let d = [a[0]-diameter/2,diameter/2+a[1]];
let aIntang = [-diameter/tang,0];
let aOuttang = [diameter/tang,0];
let bIntang = [0,-diameter/tang];
let bOuttang = [0,diameter/tang];
let cIntang = [diameter/tang,0];
let cOuttang = [-diameter/tang,0];
let dIntang = [0,diameter/tang];
let dOuttang = [0,-diameter/tang];

return createPath(points = [a, b, c, d], inTangents = [aIntang,bIntang,cIntang,dIntang],
outTangents = [aOuttang,bOuttang,cOuttang,dOuttang], is_closed = true);
}}

};

let firstCircle = new circle(thisComp.width/2,thisComp.height/2,300);

firstCircle.create();
```

We just created a circle in the middle of the composition by using an Object constructor. In this Object constructor named circle, we added x, y and diameter arguments, to which you can add a function. We added the function using the **prototype** approach, which is a way of adding a value or method to an Object constructor. We could have added it the same way as the other arguments (this.create = function()) but I wanted to show it to you this way so when you encounter it you're not lost. Now that we have an Object constructor that can generate circles, you've probably guessed that if we randomize the x and y arguments when we create the circle, it would disperse the circles on the composition when the Masks are duplicated. If you did, you're completely right but because we want to fully test the new engine, let's go even further! Let's say we want the duplicated circles to have a new position somewhere else in the composition but to never overlap each other.

Let's see step by step what we are going to add to this expression:

```
circles = [];
let i= 4000;
for (; i >= 1; i--){
EXPRESSION;
circles.push(new circle(x,y,diameter) }
```

The first thing we need to do is to create as many circles as possible thanks to the **for** loop. This loop will generate new x, y and diameters for each circle and at the end will add the new circle from the Object constructor to an Array value **circles** thanks to the **push()** method. This method can add new values to an Array when entered as arguments. The Array **circles** will contain all the circles, so circle 1 will be circles[0], circles 2 will be circles[1], etc. An Array value can contain values and also contains Objects. The first thing to notice is the variable **i** which is the number of loops that it will perform the **for** statement, which in our case is 4000. It's a lot but because we will randomize the position of the circles, we need to create enough options if we want to find position values that don't overlap since we will only keep the positions that don't overlap. If we create ten circles, and eight of them overlap with two circles, we won't end up with enough circles on the composition therefore we need a big number.

The second thing to notice is that the loop is written in reverse (instead of for(i=0;i<=4000,i++)), meaning it counts backward. This is a well-known trick to make the loop go faster. You should understand that loop statements are the most consuming calculations in Expression, we will have 4000 iterations in our loop therefore if we want good performances we now need to think about optimization.

```
let seed = i;
function random2() {
let x = Math.sin(seed++) * 10000;
return x - Math.floor(x);
};

function randomConvert(min,max){
return Math.floor(random2() * (max-min+1)+min)};

let diameter = 150;
let x = randomConvert(diameter,thisComp.width-diameter);
let y = randomConvert(diameter,thisComp.height-diameter);
```

Now we need to add a random method so that every new circle generated will have a
different position. The main issue with using the methods we know, like the **wiggle()** or
the **random()** method is that they generate different values on different properties. Even
if you use a **seedRandom()** method, we still need a random method that will create the
same value anywhere it exists. By creating a random function named **random2** using the
i variable, for each iteration we will have new values that will be the same for the 4000
iterations of every duplicated mask. However this function produces decimal Number
values between 0 and 1, if we want values that can fit in the composition we need to convert them. To do this we could have used a **linear()** method for the same result but in this
case I used a custom function so that you can see a different way of converting values
into a new range of values. Finally we created the variables that we will enter as arguments in the Object constructor based on the functions we created for the randomness.
You should also notice that we want the values to be between the diameter of the circle
and the width and height of the composition meaning the positions generated will always
be inside the composition.

```
function overlapping(x1,y1,radius1,x2,y2,radius2){
let dx = x1 - x2;
let dy = y1 - y2;
let distance = Math.sqrt(dx * dx + dy * dy);

if (distance < radius1 + radius2) {
return true;
}else{
return false};
}
```

We then need to use the function above, which basically produces a **true** value if two
circles are overlapping, otherwise it will produce a **false** value. We can't use the **length()**
method because it only gives us the distance between two points, and the circles also
have a radius to add to the distance between them.

```
total = [];
function test(x,y,diameter,theArgs) {
for (let c = theArgs.length - 1; c >= 0; c--){
let overlap = overlapping(x,y,diameter/2,theArgs[c].x,theArgs[c].y,theArgs[c].diameter/2);
if (overlap == true){
total.push(overlap);
break;};
total.push(overlap);};
```

The last function we need to add to our expression is this one above. You can see that it's a loop that uses the overlapping function we just created. Every time the loop generates a position for a new circle, this function will test the new position in every circle already created. When the new position doesn't overlap with a circle it will add a **false** value to the Array **total**. If the position overlaps with a circle, it will add a **true** value in the Array **total** then leave the loop because we don't need to test it with more circles, meaning that if the new position overlaps with one of the circles already created we don't want to use this position.

```
final = test(x,y,diameter,circles);

if (!final.includes(true)){
circles.push(new circle(x,y,diameter));
};
```

Finally we have the **if** statement. First we assign the **final** variable to the result of the previous function, which tests the new iteration with the existing circles. If you follow closely, you can see it's an Array that contains **false** and **true** values for each overlapping test it performs with circles already generated. If this Array value doesn't contain a **true** value—an overlapping—it creates the circle. If it were to contain a true value it wouldn't do anything and move to the next iteration. We're able to do this using the new **includes()** method, which checks whether the value entered as an argument in the method exists in the Array, in our case we want to know if this Array contains a **true** value. If there is one it produces a **true** value otherwise it will produce a **false** value.

```
let ind = thisProperty.propertyGroup(1).propertyIndex;
if (circles.length - 1 == ind) {break;}
```

Finally, as I mentioned the loop statements are the most consuming calculations in Expression, and you want to avoid having as many loops as possible. When using this **if** statement, if the Array Index number of the circle generated has the same number as the Index number of the Mask group in the hierarchy, it leaves the loop. So for example when it produces the circle 2 on Mask 2 it won't calculate the following circles. Doing this will avoid unnecessary calculations which means better performances.

```
/* FUNCTION OVERLAPPING */
function overlapping(x1,y1,radius1,x2,y2,radius2){
let dx = x1 - x2;
let dy = y1 - y2;
let distance = Math.sqrt(dx * dx + dy * dy);
if (distance < radius1 + radius2) {
return true;
}else{
return false};}

/* OBJECT CONSTRUCTOR */
function circle(x,y,diameter) {
    this.x = x;
    this.y = y;
    this.diameter = diameter;
{
circle.prototype.create = function() {
let positionCircle = [this.x,this.y];
let diameter = this.diameter;
const tang = 3.8;
let a = [positionCircle[0],positionCircle[1]-diameter/2];
let b = [diameter/2+a[0],diameter/2+a[1]];
let c = [a[0],diameter+a[1]];
let d = [a[0]-diameter/2,diameter/2+a[1]];
let aIntang = [-diameter/tang,0];
let aOuttang = [diameter/tang,0];
let bIntang = [0,-diameter/tang];
let bOuttang = [0,diameter/tang];
let cIntang = [diameter/tang,0];
let cOuttang = [-diameter/tang,0];
let dIntang = [0,diameter/tang];
let dOuttang = [0,-diameter/tang];

return createPath(points=[a,b,c,d],inTangents=[aIntang,bIntang,cIntang,dIntang],
outTangents = [aOuttang,bOuttang,cOuttang,dOuttang], is_closed = true);}}}
let ind = thisProperty.propertyGroup(1).propertyIndex

/* EXPRESSION */
circles = [];
let i= 4000;

for (; i >= 1; i--){
let seed = i;
function random2() {
let x = Math.sin(seed++) * 10000;
return x - Math.floor(x);
};
```

```javascript
function randomConvert(min,max){
    return Math.floor(random2() * (max-min+1)+min)};

let diameter = 150;
let x = randomConvert(diameter,thisComp.width-diameter);
let y = randomConvert(diameter,thisComp.height-diameter);

total = [];
function test(x,y,diameter,theArgs) {
for (let c = theArgs.length - 1; c >= 0; c--){
let overlap = overlapping(x,y,diameter/2,theArgs[c].x,theArgs[c].y,theArgs[c].
diameter/2);
if (overlap == true){
total.push(overlap);
break;};
total.push(overlap);};

return total;};

final = test(x,y,diameter,circles);
if (!final.includes(true)){
circles.push(new circle(x,y,diameter)); };

if (circles.length - 1 == ind) {break;}  };

circles[ind].create();
```

Now let's duplicate the Mask about 20 times and see the result.

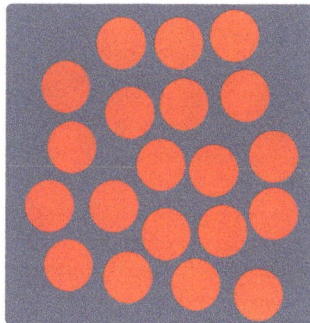

👁	▼ ■ 1	■ SOLID LAYER			
	▼ Masks				
	► ■ Mask 1	Add	✓	Inverted
	► ■ Mask 2	Add	✓	Inverted
	► ■ Mask 3	Add	✓	Inverted
	► ■ Mask 4	Add	✓	Inverted
	► ■ Mask 5	Add	✓	Inverted
	► ■ Mask 6	Add	✓	Inverted
	► ■ Mask 7	Add	✓	Inverted
	► ■ Mask 8	Add	✓	Inverted
	► ■ Mask 9	Add	✓	Inverted
	► ■ Mask 10	Add	✓	Inverted
	► ■ Mask 11	Add	✓	Inverted
	► ■ Mask 12	Add	✓	Inverted
	► ■ Mask 13	Add	✓	Inverted
	► ■ Mask 14	Add	✓	Inverted
	► ■ Mask 15	Add	✓	Inverted
	► ■ Mask 16	Add	✓	Inverted
	► ■ Mask 17	Add	✓	Inverted
	► ■ Mask 18	Add	✓	Inverted
	► ■ Mask 19	Add	✓	Inverted
	► ■ Mask 20	Add	✓	Inverted

It works well and it's also pretty responsive. We can see that if we keep duplicating more circles we end up with an error, that's because if we want more circles, we have to create more options meaning more iterations. To do this you just have increase the number of loop iterations to a higher number. But in our example we will stay at 4000. The great thing about the Object constructor, is that everything depends only on one expression. Let's say that you want to change something, you can simply delete all of the duplicated masks and edit the expression in Mask 1, then duplicate it again. For example, we could have also randomized the diameter of the circle with the same random function.

```
let diameter = randomConvert(50,250);
```

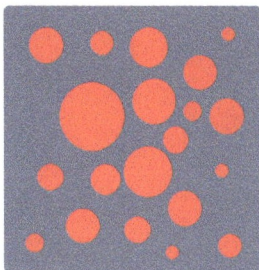

Now to push the engine a little bit more I would like to add one last condition, I would like for circles only to exist inside a path. Add a new Blue solid layer and draw a circle mask in it.

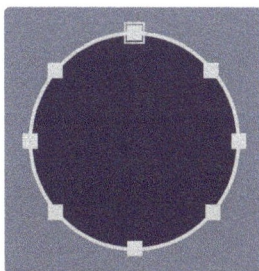

We are going to use this path as the shape in which we will insert our circles. We could have used any kind of shape. Whether you decide to have a circle shape like mine or something else, make sure you add plenty of points on the path, it will be more precise for the expressions engine. Now let's edit our expression. Let's add a variable that stores the values of the points of this path:

```
const shape = thisComp.layer("Blue Solid 1").mask("Mask 1").maskPath.points();
```

Now we have to add one more function to make this happen. We need a function that can state whether a point (x,y) is inside a path:

```
function inside(point, path) {
let x = point[0], y = point[1];
let inside = false;
for (let i = 0, j = path.length - 1; i < path.length; j = i++) {
let xi = path[i][0], yi = path[i][1];
let xj = path[j][0], yj = path[j][1];
let intersect = ((yi > y) != (yj > y)) && (x < (xj - xi) * (y - yi) / (yj - yi) + xi);
if (intersect) inside = !inside;
}
return inside;
};
```

When we insert the x and y position generated by the main loop as the first argument and the **shape** variable we created as second argument, the function tells us whether or not the point is inside the path. Knowing this, with a simple **if** statement when the function produces **true** it can create a new circle, otherwise it doesn't do anything and starts a new iteration.

```
resArrX = [];
resArrY = [];

for(let t = 0; t < shape.length; t++){
let d = shape[t][0];
resArrX.push(d);
};
for(let t = 0; t < shape.length; t++){
let d = shape[t][1];
resArrY.push(d);
};

let minX = Math.min(...resArrX);
let maxX = Math.max(...resArrX);
let minY = Math.min(...resArrY);
let maxY = Math.max(...resArrY);
```

Last but not least, we want to limit the iterations so that values are only created in the area where the shape is, therefore it increases the number of options to find circles that exist inside the path. Otherwise the loop could generate circle positions that exist outside of this area but since we don't need them, those iterations would be useless. By adding this to the expression, it can locate which are the minimum and maximum values of the shape on x and y—therefore limiting the area where the positions are generated.
You can note that for this we used the spread operators which really allows us to avoid extra-steps. Finally, we can implement this to our variables:

```
let diameter = randomConvert(10,200);
let x = randomConvert(diameter+minX,maxX-diameter);
let y = randomConvert(diameter+minY,maxY-diameter);
```

So here is the final expression:

```
/* FUNCTION INSIDE */
function inside(point, path) {
let x = point[0], y = point[1];
let inside = false;
for (let i = 0, j = path.length - 1; i < path.length; j = i++) {
let xi = path[i][0], yi = path[i][1];
let xj = path[j][0], yj = path[j][1];
let intersect = ((yi > y) != (yj > y)) && (x < (xj - xi) * (y - yi) / (yj - yi) + xi);
if (intersect) inside = !inside;
}
return inside;
};

const shape = thisComp.layer("Blue Solid 1").mask("Mask 1").maskPath.points();

/* FUNCTION OVERLAPPING */
function overlapping(x1,y1,radius1,x2,y2,radius2){
let dx = x1 - x2;
let dy = y1 - y2;
let distance = Math.sqrt(dx * dx + dy * dy);
if (distance < radius1 + radius2) {
return true;
}else{
return false};
}

/* BOUNDARIES SHAPE */
resArrX = [];
resArrY = [];
for(let t = 0; t < shape.length; t++){
let d = shape[t][0];
resArrX.push(d);
};
for(let t = 0; t < shape.length; t++){
let d = shape[t][1];
```

```
resArrY.push(d);
};
let minX = Math.min(...resArrX);
let maxX = Math.max(...resArrX);
let minY = Math.min(...resArrY);
let maxY = Math.max(...resArrY);

/* OBJECT CONSTRUCTOR */
function circle(x,y,diameter) {
    this.x = x;
    this.y = y;
    this.diameter = diameter;
{
circle.prototype.create = function() {
let positionCircle = [this.x,this.y];
let diameter = this.diameter;
const tang = 3.8;
let a = [positionCircle[0],positionCircle[1]-diameter/2];
let b = [diameter/2+a[0],diameter/2+a[1]];
let c = [a[0],diameter+a[1]];
let d = [a[0]-diameter/2,diameter/2+a[1]];
let aIntang = [-diameter/tang,0];
let aOuttang = [diameter/tang,0];
let bIntang = [0,-diameter/tang];
let bOuttang = [0,diameter/tang];
let cIntang = [diameter/tang,0];
let cOuttang = [-diameter/tang,0];
let dIntang = [0,diameter/tang];
let dOuttang = [0,-diameter/tang];

return createPath(points=[a,b,c,d],inTangents=[aIntang,bIntang,cIntang,dIntang],
outTangents = [aOuttang,bOuttang,cOuttang,dOuttang], is_closed = true); }}}

let ind = thisProperty.propertyGroup(1).propertyIndex;

/* EXPRESSION */
circles = [];
Iterations = 4000;
for (let i= 0; i < Iterations; ++i){
let seed = i;

function random2() {
let x = Math.sin(seed++) * 10000;
return x - Math.floor(x);
};

function randomConvert(min,max){
return Math.floor(random2() * (max-min+1)+min)};

let diameter = randomConvert(50,200);
let x = randomConvert(diameter+minX,maxX-diameter);
```

```
let y = randomConvert(diameter+minY,maxY-diameter);

total = [];
function test(x,y,diameter,theArgs) {
for (let c = theArgs.length - 1; c >= 0; c--){
let overlap = overlapping(x,y,diameter/2,theArgs[c].x,theArgs[c].y,theArgs[c].
diameter/2);
if (overlap == true){
total.push(overlap);
break;};
total.push(overlap);};
return total;};

if (inside([x,y],shape)){
final = test(x,y,diameter,circles);
if (!final.includes(true)){
circles.push(new circle(x,y,diameter));
};
}

if (circles.length - 1 == ind) {break;} };

circles[ind].create();
```

If we duplicate Mask 1, about 20 times we can see it works well and still acts pretty responsive. Also, if we modify the path of the shape we can see it automatically updates and the circles are distributed inside the new shape.

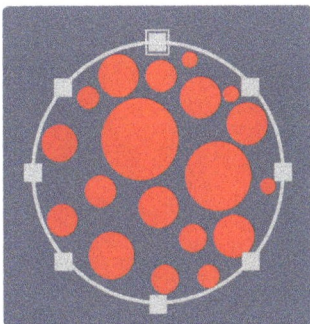

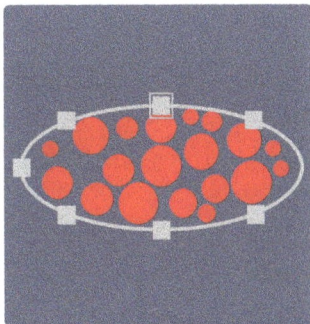

After running this test, you'll be surprised to find that by using the new engine and its new tools along with practicing good habits, the calculations to produce this advanced expression will take up to about 11 seconds. If we were to try making a similar expression in the old engine, without the new terms, the calculations for this would have lasted up to 4 minutes. It's a significant difference. We can see that thanks to this new engine, we can go even further and have even more control and influence in our expressions.

Built-In Terms:
Object / Value

thisProject — fullPath
linearBlending
bitsPerChannel

comp() or — numLayers   displayStartTime   name
thisComp   activeCamera   frameDuration   layer()
            width   shutterAngle   layerByComment()
            height   shutterPhase   marker
            duration   bgColor
            ntscDropFrame   pixelAspect

layer() or — name   rotationX   timeToNTSCTimecode()   timeRemap
thisLayer   numEntries   rotationY   timeToCurrentFormat()   motionTracker
            numProperties   rotationZ   seedRandom()   transform
            active   castsShadows   random()   layerStyle
            enabled   lightTransmission   gaussRandom()   geometryOption
            thisComp   acceptsShadows   noise()   materialOption
            thisProject   acceptsLights   degreesToRadians()   audio
            time   ambient   radiansToDegrees()   masterProperty
            colorDepth   diffuse   linear()   text
            source   specularIntensity   ease()
            width   specularShininess   easeIn()
            height   metal   easeOut()
            index   comp()   rgbToHsl()
            parent   footage()   hslToRgb()
            hasParent   posterizeTime()   hexToRgb()
            inPoint   add()   sampleImage()
            outPoint   sub()   effect()
            startTime   mul()   mask()
            hasVideo   div()   sourceRectAtTime()
            hasAudio   clamp()   sourceTime()
            audioActive   length()   toComp()
            anchorPoint   dot()   fromComp()
            position   normalize()   toWorld()
            scale   cross()   fromWorld()
            rotation   lookAt()   toCompVec()
            opacity   timeToFrames()   fromCompVec()
            audioLevels   framesToTime()   toWorldVec()
            timeRemap   timeToTimecode()   fromWorldVec()
            marker   timeToFeetAndFrames()   fromCompToSurface()
            orientation   marker

anchorPoint
position

position	value	enabled	speedAtTime()	loopInDuration()
scale	velocity	propertyIndex	wiggle()	loopOutDuration()
rotation	speed	toString()	temporalWiggle()	key()
opacity	numKeys	valueOf()	smooth()	nearestKey()
param()	name	valueAtTime()	loopIn()	propertyGroup()
or any other	active	velocityAtTime()	loopOut()	
properties in AE				

Math

cos()	exp()	floor()	LOG10E
acos()	pow()	min()	LN2
tan()	log()	max()	LN10
atan()	abs()	PI	SQRT2
sin()	round()	E	SQRT1_2
sqrt()	ceil()	LOG2E	

footage()

width	ntscDropFrame	sourceData	dataValue()
height	pixelAspect	dataKeyValues()	
duration	name	dataKeyTimes()	
frameDuration	sourceText	dataKeyCount()	

text.sourceText

value	charAt()	search()	toUpperCase()
numKeys	charCodeAt()	slice()	
name	fromCharCode()	split()	
active	valueAtTime()	substr()	
enabled	indexOf()	substring()	
propertyIndex	lastIndexOf()	propertyGroup()	
length	localeCompare()	key()	
toString()	match()	nearestKey()	
valueOf()	replace()	toLowerCase()	

effect()

name	numProperties	active	param()
numEntries	propertyIndex	enabled	

marker.key()

value	chapter	eventCuePoint	valueOf()
time	url	cuePointName	toString()
index	frameTarget	parameters	
comment	protectedRegion	duration	

key()

value	index	toString()
time	valueOf()	

sourceRectAtTime()

top	width
left	height

Tell me how You really feel:

thepowerofexpression@outlook.com

Thanks to:
Andy Redwood
Reynald Philippe
Melissa Espinosa
My family and friends
Adobe and its developers
The After Effects community
Lloyd Alvarez and AESCRIPTS
Coworkers I've met during my career

www.ingramcontent.com/pod-product-compliance
Lightning Source LLC
Chambersburg PA
CBHW051125210326

41458CB00067B/6237